GOVERNORS STATE UNIVERSITY LIBRARY

W9-CMU-560
3 1611 00104 1455

WITHDRAWN

A Hispanic Heritage

*A guide to juvenile books
about Hispanic people and cultures*

Isabel Schon

UNIVERSITY LIBRARY
GOVERNORS STATE UNIVERSITY
PARK FOREST SOUTH, ILL.

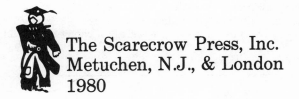
The Scarecrow Press, Inc.
Metuchen, N.J., & London
1980

OTHER SCARECROW TITLES BY
ISABEL SCHON

A Bicultural Heritage
Books in Spanish for Children and Young Adults

Library of Congress Cataloging in Publication Data

Schon, Isabel.
  A Hispanic heritage.

  Includes indexes.
  1. Latin America--Juvenile literature--Bibliography.
2. Spain--Juvenile literature--Bibliography. I. Title.
Z1609.C5S36   016.98   80-10935
ISBN 0-8108-1290-8

Copyright © 1980 by Isabel Schon

Manufactured in the United States of America

Z
1609
.C5
S36

UNIVERSITY LIBRARY
GOVERNORS STATE UNIVERSITY
PARK FOREST SOUTH, ILL.

ACKNOWLEDGMENTS

I would like to express my sincere appreciation to the many wonderful people who assisted me in the preparation of this book. I am indebted to Ms. Barbara Quarles for her endless search of books; to Ms. Stephanie Reith and to Mrs. Bonnie Halfpenny for their suggestions and recommendations; to Mrs. Elizabeth Outcalt for her usual kindnesses; and to the following librarians who always cheerfully helped me with their superior knowledge and efficiency: Mrs. Vida Bernard, Mrs. Jane Cox, Ms. Susan Garvin, Ms. Donna Larson, Mrs. Melva McClellan, Mrs. Alida Stevens, Mrs. Lyle Watrous, and many others.

I also wish to express my gratitude to my husband, Dr. R. R. Chalquest, and to my daughter, Verita, for their patience, understanding, and loving support, and to the Faculty Research Grant Committee, College of Education, Arizona State University for making this work possible.

iii

TABLE OF CONTENTS

PREFACE

A Hispanic Heritage is designed as
an aid for librarians and teachers who are
interested in exposing students to the cultures of Hispanic people through books for
children and adolescents.

These books are intended to provide
students in kindergarten through high school
with an understanding of, and an appreciation for, the people, history, art, and political, social, and economic problems of
Argentina, Chile, Colombia, Cuba, Mexico,
Panama, Peru, Puerto Rico, Spain, Venezuela, and the Hispanic-heritage people in
the United States.

A Hispanic Heritage is arranged into
chapters that explore specific countries and
cultures, as well as one on Latin America
as a whole. The books are listed in alpha-
betical order by author surname. These
countries are representative of Hispanic cultures and should assist librarians, teachers,
and students in their efforts to better know
and comprehend the marvelous richness and
diversity of the cultures of Hispanic people.

Although I have attempted to include
most in-print books in English published in
the United States that relate to the countries
and people listed above, as well as general
books on Latin America, I undoubtedly have

vii

missed some important books. Their omis-
sion is due to unavailability, nonexistence at
the time of compilation, or my own lack of
awareness of them. However, not all the
books listed are recommended titles. For
the convenience of the reader, I have marked
with an asterisk (*) noteworthy books. These
books contain recent information, as well as
being entertaining with a high potential for
interesting or involving the reader. I urge
readers to be especially critical of many
books that contain obsolete information or
that expose a very limited or one-sided view
of Hispanic people, customs, or countries.
Students should be encouraged to read books
that provide objective information and that
present new insights into Hispanic people
and cultures.

As any librarian or teacher knows,
it is very difficult to assign a grade level
to a book. And, even though I have done
so for the convenience of some teachers or
students, please use the grade level only as
a tentative guideline. An arbitrary grade
level should never stop a student from reading or viewing a book that he or she expresses interest in.

In the annotations I have expressed
my personal opinions of the books, emphasizing what I believe are the strengths or
weaknesses of each. I have summarized,
criticized, and/or highlighted specific ideas
explored in the books about Hispanic countries and people.

In anticipation of user needs I have
provided three indexes: the author index;
the subject index, including references and
cross-references; and the title index.

It is my hope that A Hispanic Heritage will encourage readers, librarians, teachers, and even publishers to expand their interests into the fascinating cultures of Hispanic people both in the United States and abroad.

A HISPANIC HERITAGE:

A Guide to Juvenile Books
About Hispanic People and Cultures

LATIN AMERICA

Latin America begins south of the United States. It includes half the area of the Western Hemisphere and about half the total population. Latin America is also known as Spanish America, Hispanic America, Ibero-America, and Indo-America. These terms come from the origins of its inhabitants: Spain, the Iberian Peninsula (Spain and Portugal), and Indo (Pre-Columbian Indians).

There are many similarities and differences among Latin American people. Some of the similarities include:

- a common cultural heritage from Mediterranean Europe
- a similar colonial experience
- the majority of the people are Catholic
- the majority of the inhabitants are racially mixed.

Some of the differences are:

- the Brazilians speak Portuguese; the Haitians, French; and most other Latin American people, Spanish
- in Argentina and Uruguay the people are predominantly white
- great differences in the physical features and natural resources in the various countries have resulted in many differences in the level of economic growth and cultural development of the people.

3

Pre-Columbian civilizations achieved various levels of cultural development. The Mayas, the Aztecs, and the Incas produced outstanding civilizations. They constructed large cities with imposing architectural styling, organized empires, acquired a knowledge of mathematics and astronomy, utilized forms of writing, and worked in precious stones, metals, and gems.

The Spanish conquest was completed in a period of approximately eighty years, and its absolute authority endured nearly three hundred years. Spain's objectives were mainly to spread the Catholic faith and to extract wealth for shipment to the homeland. During the colonial period Spanish government was highly centralized, with most power held by an absolute monarch. Little thought was given to the settlement of the land, or to the future development of industry and trade.

Latin Americans have excelled in several of the arts. Since the sixteenth century elaborate churches have displayed the Indian craftspeople's interpretation of European style. Mexico's dramatic and colorful murals and frescoes, which deal chiefly with social and historical themes, are world famous. Latin American music, which is gay and lively, is one of the continent's biggest exports. Many Latin American writers are read all over the world, such as Gabriela Mistral, Miguel Angel Asturias, Pablo Neruda, Octavio Paz, and Gabriel García Márquez.

Today Latin American nations face many problems: widespread poverty, hunger, illiteracy and disease, as well as one-product economies that suffer from fluctuations of prices in world markets and underdeveloped social and political systems. These problems seem to merge in the triple threat of constantly increasing populations, severe pollution, and dangerously high unemployment rates. As a result, Latin American cities are becoming more crowded, jobs more difficult to find, traffic more jammed, food more expensive, skies more polluted, educational opportunities increasingly scarce, and water less available.

The following books provide an interesting introduction to Latin America from a historical, geographical, and political perspective.   (Asterisks indicate noteworthy books.)

Bailey, Bernadine.   Famous Latin-American Liberators.
Illus. :   Gerald McCann.   (New York: Dodd, Mead &
Company, 1960, 153 p.)   Grades: 7-9.

    This is a collection of ten brief biographies of
the following heroes of Latin America narrated in approximately ten pages each: Francisco de Miranda
(1756-1816), Simón Bolívar (1783-1830), Antonio José
de Sucre (1795-1830), José de San Martín (1778-1850),
Bernardo O'Higgins (1778-1842), Miguel Hidalgo y Cos-
tilla (1753-1811), José María Morelos (1765-1815),
Benito Pablo Juárez (1806-1872), José Julian Martí
(1853-1895), Toussaint L'Ouverture (1744-1803).   The
brevity of these accounts perhaps compelled the author
to sensationalize some of her quotes, such as the one
she attributes to Simón Bolívar during his campaign in
Peru: "'We must liberate these people in spite of
themselves....   Otherwise we shall be campaigning to
the end of the world'" (p.   40).

Baker, Nina Brown.   He Wouldn't Be King: The Story
of Simón Bolívar.   Illus. :   Camilo Egas.   (New York:
The Vanguard Press, 1941, 300 p.)   Grades: 7-12.

    Through the life of Simón Bolívar, the Liberator
of Venezuela, Colombia, Ecuador, Peru, and Bolivia,
the reader is introduced to important differences between the North American and South American colonies
in the early nineteenth century.   The author narrates
very simply many personal incidents in Bolívar's private
and political life that serve to increase the reader's understanding of his motivations, achievements, and dilemmas.   In trying to explain many differences between
American and Spanish customs, the author describes a
practice that is now outdated, but which she represents
as still prevailing "among conservative Spanish fam-

ilies....   A girl who is old enough to marry, among
the Spanish people, is far too young and giddy to make
a proper choice....   Her parents, with the wisdom of
age, know best those sterling qualities which make for
a happy married life, and they would consider themselves unfit for parenthood if they failed to protect their
daughters by the exercise of their superior judgment....
Harsh though it seems to North Americans, it does not
work out too badly.   There are few old maids in such
families, and no divorces" (p. 27).

Baum, Patricia.   Dictators of Latin America.   (New
York: G. P. Putnam's Sons, 1972, 186 p.)   Grades:
6-12.

        Through the lives of seven Latin American dic-
tators, the author proposed to explore "the phenomenon
of Latin American dictatorship. "   What the author did
achieve is her own interpretation of the origins of dictatorship (which some historians would call realistic)
and her own views of "good" and "bad" Latin American
dictators (which most Latin Americans would call ridiculous).   The dictators and the author's subtitles are:
Porfirio Díaz: Maker of Millionaires and Misery;
Rafael Trujillo: Butcher of the Caribbean; Getúlio Vargas: Father of Modern Brazil; Perón and Eva: The
Husband-Wife Team; Alfredo Stroessner: Caudillo
Turned Modern Ruler; Papa Doc: The Voodoo Tyrant;
and Fidel Castro: The Red Revolutionary.
        Many Latin American scholars would object to
this author's verdicts such as, "Besides a need to show
off, Trujillo had a great compulsion to prove his super-
human Latin machismo, his maleness.   Although he
was married--three times in fact--he had countless
mistresses, plus hundreds of one-time 'conquests'" (p.
51).
        The author asserts that Stroessner "has changed
and has gradually become a more modern ruler in re-
sponse to the new forces that are at work today in
Latin America" (pp. 110-112).
        And, the author's decree regarding Castro: "He
was a dictator committed to a totalitarian movement that

aimed to destroy freedom throughout the hemisphere"
(p. 151). Perhaps this author should limit her writings
to her own sphere of knowledge and leave Latin America to authors who are more willing to do their home-
work.

Borreson, Mary Jo.   Let's Go to South America.   Illus. : Jane Evans.   (New York: G. P. Putnam's Sons,
1969, 45 p.) Grades: 3-6.

    Simple text and appropriate line drawings very
briefly describe important characteristics of the thirteen South American countries.   There are eight pages
devoted to the Incas; nine pages tell about Brazil; and
a few paragraphs mention Ecuador, Bolivia, and Uruguay.   Nevertheless, the author highlighted very well
the key characteristics of each country.   There are a
few statements that contain outdated information: "Venezuela produces more oil than any other country in the
world" (p. 42).   And, "the Organization of American
States and the Alliance for Progress are working together to help the people of all the American countries
improve the conditions of our friends to the south" (p.
45).

Carter, William E.   The First Book of South America.
Rev. ed.   (New York: Franklin Watts, 1972, 86 p.)
Grades: 4-6.

    Simply and briefly the author introduces the land,
history, culture, industries, and people of the thirteen
countries of South America.   There are very interesting
comparisons of the Spanish and Portuguese settlements
in South America in the sixteenth century.   The author
describes the Spaniards' and Portuguese's eagerness to
live like aristocrats: "The Spaniards found this way of
life easy to achieve.   On the west coast were the Inca
Empire and the Chibcha chiefdoms.   Each of these con-
tained large numbers of Indians who were used to long,
hard hours of labor, and to taking orders from lords
and princes" (p. 4).   "Early Spanish settlers in the

Andes were fortunate not only in finding a good labor force; they also discovered large deposits of gold and silver.   The early Portuguese found nothing like this in the lands assigned to them ... most of the Indians they met either refused to work, ran away, or grew sick and died.   To solve their problem, they finally decided to look elsewhere, and they began to import black slaves from Africa" (pp. 5 and 6).

*Fisher, John R.   Latin America from Conquest to Independence.   (New York: The John Day Company, 1971, 125 p.)   Grades: 9-12.

This is an excellent survey of Spanish and Portuguese America from the beginning of colonization in the late fifteenth century to the early nineteenth century, when all the mainland colonies secured their independence.   In an easy-to-understand manner the author highlights Latin America's important historical events and economic factors and relationship with Spain and Portugal.   Spain's influences, as well as its internal problems as they affected Latin America, are especially well explained.   In the postscript the author describes his realistic view of Latin America in the nineteenth and twentieth centuries: "As far as the structure of society was concerned, the wars of independence simply transferred power from a selfish Spanish minority to a selfish creole minority" (p. 118).   And, "Although the Latin American states seized political independence from Spain and Portugal in the early nineteenth century, they did not become economically free.   They became dependent upon Britain in the nineteenth century, and today they are dependent upon North America.   In this economic sense they are still colonies" (p. 121).

Goetz, Delia.   Neighbors to the South.   (New York: Harcourt, Brace & World, 1956, 163 p.)   Grades: 7-9.

This book was meant to be an introduction to Latin American countries in the 1940s and then updated with information from the 1950 census.   It briefly (in

four or five pages) describes each of the Island Repub-
lics, Mexico, the Central American, and the South
American countries.   It also tells about the trade, artists, education, and heroes of Latin America.   However, the obsolete information recounted as well as the
outdated photographs make this book of very little value.   For example, the latest information about the
Panama Canal refers to the 1936 U. S. yearly payments:
"By terms of a new treaty in 1936 this was increased
to $430, 000" (p. 57).

It mentions the "modern" inventions that brought
changes to Argentina.   It describes wire fences, ma-
chines for harvesting and threshing grain and, "another
invention significant for Argentina was refrigeration"
(p. 95).   Yes, these inventions were modern in the 1940s!

It still cites Rio de Janeiro as the capital of
Brazil, and so on.

Joy, Charles R.   Getting to Know the River Amazon.
Illus. :   Nathan Goldstein.   (New York: Coward-Mc-
Cann, 1963, 61 p.)   Grades: 3-5.

Neither the awkward illustrations nor the stilted
text in this book convey the true marvels of the Amazon
River.   Very superficially the author tells about the
sources of the Amazon in the Peruvian Andes, remote
Indian villages and delta rubber farms, wild beasts and
insects of the jungle, and Indian multi-family homes.
Many pages are devoted to dull descriptions of agen-
cies, countries, or private groups that are providing
money or experts "to help the people of the Amazon
basin develop its resources" (p. 53).   So, young readers are supposed to be interested in the work of such
organizations as the Central Baptist Foundation, the
Wycliffe Bible Translators, the Organization of American States, and the International Basic Economy Corporation, and their "wonderful" achievements in the Amazon.

May, Charles Paul.   Peru, Bolivia, Ecuador: the Indian Andes.   (New Jersey: Thomas Nelson, 1969, 211
p.)   Grades: 7-12.

This is a very readable account of the history, the economic and political problems, and the people of Peru, Bolivia, and Ecuador. The author should be commended for his realistic report of the conditions and problems that these countries face; however, he seems to have received most of his information from Peace Corps volunteers, as these are the only ones that receive any credit for trying to improve the life of the people. The author is quite pessimistic about these countries' future, and unfortunately, most economists would agree with the author's conclusions: "It is not enough to say something should be done for the poor. Action must be taken. But the well-to-do people of the central Andes fear action that will improve conditions for people who have long been held down.... So talk goes on while little gets done" (p. 207).

The author, unfortunately, is too quick in reporting some obvious misrepresentations or misunderstandings about the way of life of middle- or upper-class families in Latin America. Regarding family life and customs in the central Andes, the author mistakenly states that "no parent in the middle or upper classes would think of punishing a child. It has been said, and not entirely as a joke, that among upper-class families a man is more likely to strike his wife than his child" (p. 138). Wrong, wrong, wrong on all counts!

Nevins, Albert J.   Away to the Lands of the Andes. (New York: Dodd, Mead & Company, 1962, 95 p.) Grades 5-8.

Students of religious history might be interested in this book about Colombia, Ecuador, Peru, Bolivia, and Chile, which was copyrighted in 1962 by the Catholic Foreign Mission Society of America, Inc. Very briefly and simply the author, Father Nevins, describes the history, geography, and problems of these five Andean countries from a Catholic perspective. He emphasizes the sacrifices that were made by the priests during colonial times, as well as the problems that the Catholic Church encountered in these Andean countries after their independence from Spain. The author explains the

problems of many Indians again from his point of view:
"Few Indian villages have resident priests. . . . If they
are very lucky, they may have a priest to offer Mass
on the day of their village fiesta. The fiesta is a break
in their monotonous lives. While it is often marked by
drunkenness and debauchery, the Indian should not be
too greatly blamed. Where there is religious care and
the Indian is educated in his religion, he leads a very
moral life and is devoted to his church" (pp. 78-79).

*Perry, Roger. Patagonia: Windswept Land of the South.
(New York: Dodd, Mead & Company, 1974, 117 p.)
Grades: 6-12.

This is an enthusiastic and simply written description of Patagonia, "the region at the far south of the
American continent. It is shared between Argentina and
Chile and runs at its tip into the bleak archipelago known
as Tierra del Fuego" (p. 11). Black-and-white photographs complement the text, which describes the beauties
of the Strait of Magellan, the eastern steppes, fiords, and
glaciers, and the emerging Patagonia, as well as making
brief historical references to the early peoples and the
first explorers. The author's great joy in writing about
his travels to this region is evident throughout the book.
The following is a short example of his description of the
Muñoz Gamero Peninsula: "In the morning the clouds
parted and I had my first glimpse of the haunting beauty
of the region. The mirror-calm sea and nearby slopes
were bathed in sunlight. The clouds, even as they cleared,
were suffused with soft pastel colors which matched the
tranquility of the scene. . . " (p. 18).

*Prago, Albert. The Revolutions in Spanish America:
The Independence Movements of 1808-1825. (New York:
The Macmillan Company, 1970, 226 p.) Grades: 9-12.

In a very simple, readable manner the author
traces the historical background and the causes of the
wars for independence of the Spanish-speaking nations of
the Western Hemisphere. He stresses an important fact
regarding the economic situation in the Spanish-speaking

colonies: ". . . at the time of the outbreak of the wars
for independence the colonies were enjoying relative
prosperity . . . the creoles--and some others--believed
that they could do much better without the heavy presence of imperialist Spain" (pp. 32-33).

The author describes Mexico's independence from
Spain and describes its results: "Release from the
burdens of imperial Spanish rule did not produce freedom for Indians and Negroes. . . .   The status of the
church remained fundamentally the same; if anything,
its power and wealth increased. . . .   The new chief power was the army, upon whose support the government
and the church rested. . . .   For more than fifty years
Mexico was to be convulsed with civil war, anarchy, and
revolution" (p. 107).   There are brief accounts of Latin
America's heroes, such as Bolívar, Hidalgo, Morelos,
O'Higgins, and San Martín.   However, the author's
skepticism regarding the independence movements in
Latin America are summed up in his own final ques-
tions: "Should the colonial emancipations be viewed as
inconsequential events insofar as the history of freedom
is concerned?   Must one come to the pessimistic, skep-
tical conclusion that the emancipation of nations is vain
and futile if their peoples are not free?" (pp. 225-226).

*Prieto, Mariana.   Play It in Spanish.   Illus.:   Regina
and Haig Sherkerjian.   (New York: The John Day Company, 1973, 43 p.)   Grades: K-2.

Collection of seventeen well-known Latin American and Spanish games and nursery songs that will appeal to all children who are familiar with the Spanish
language, especially children who have a Hispanic heritage.   It includes the music for the songs and the words
in Spanish with a free English translation.

Quinn, Vernon.   Picture Map Geography of Mexico, Central America, and the West Indies.   Illus.:   Da Osimo.
(New York: J. B. Lippincott Company, [revised 1963]
1943, 114 p.)   Grades: 4-6.

I am inclined to disbelieve the publisher's claim
that this book was revised in 1963.   It includes brief
descriptions of the countries in Central America, the
West Indies, and Mexico with much obsolete information.   For example, it states: "Mexico, the capital,
is the largest city in the republic, with five and a half
million inhabitants, a great number of them being Indians. ...   When the Indians have anything for sale, their
wares are spread out in neat little piles on the pave-
ment and may be purchased for a copper centavo or
two" (p. 12).   This is truly a ludicrous description of
Mexico City.   Again; "Belize is the only country in
Central America that is not a Latin-American Republic.
It is a British Crown Colony" (p. 28).   And, the most
recent information about Cuba is: "The leading export
is sugar, and more sugar and more sugar." " (p. 92).
   Dainty "Curio-type" designs complement each
country.

*Rink, Paul.   Soldier of the Andes: José de San Martín.
(New York: Julian Messner, 1971, 182 p.)   Grades:
7-12.

   This is a very well written biography of José de
San Martín, the general who led the war for independence in Argentina and who also participated in the liberation of Chile and Peru.   San Martín's political and
military careers are interestingly described.   However,
there are very few references made about his personal
life.   San Martín's unfortunate and controversial need
for opium to relieve his suffering from the pain caused
by ulcers is mentioned several times: "In those days
little was known about his malady.   There was only one
known remedy: something to kill the pain.   In San
Martín's case, this continued to be ever-increasing
dosages of opium.   In order to keep going he was by
now taking the drug in such quantities that its effects
were debilitating and stupefying" (p. 106).
   San Martín's genius as a military commander
and his honesty and dedication to the cause of freedom
from the Spaniards in South America are very well explained.   The author is an obvious admirer of San

Martín: "There was a nobility and a grandeur ... that
set him centuries ahead of all those about him and
raised him to a plane reserved for very few men" (p.
145).

*Selsam, Millicent E. , editor.   Stars, Mosquitoes, and
Crocodiles: The American Travels of Alexander Von
Humboldt.   Illus.:   Russell Francis Peterson.   (New
York: Harper & Row, 1962, 166 p.)   Grades: 7-12.

     This book contains marvelously edited and
abridged selections of Alexander Von Humboldt's travels
in South America, Cuba, Mexico, and the United States
from 1799 to 1804.   All readers will be fascinated by
Humboldt's amazing scientific investigations, as well as
his personal observations of life in America in the early
1800s.   The editor's interesting notes and the attractive
black-and-white drawings and maps complement Humboldt's exciting narrative, which should enthrall nature
lovers and would-be historians.   The following are Humboldt's personal reactions after a long and tiring journey:
"The inconveniences endured at sea in small vessels
are trivial in comparison with those that are suffered
under a burning sky, surrounded by swarms of mosquitoes and lying stretched in a canoe without the pos-
sibility of taking the least bodily exercise....   We admired the conveniences which industry and commerce
furnish to civilized man.   Humble dwellings appeared to
us magnificent, and every person with whom we con-
versed seemed to be endowed with superior intelligence.
Long privations give a value to the smallest enjoyments,
and I cannot express the pleasure we felt when we first
saw wheat bread on the governor's table" (p. 101).

Syme, Ronald.   Bolívar: The Liberator.   Illus.:   William Stobbs.   (New York: William Morrow and Company, 1968, 190 p.)   Grades: 5-9.

     This is a simply written biography of Simón
Bolívar.   It describes Bolívar as a young multimillion-
aire and member of one of Venezuela's most influential

families, his experiences in Europe, his dedication to his ideal to unify and to free South America from Spain, and his death in Santa Marta.   Perhaps the author felt compelled to judge Bolívar's actions: Bolívar's "weakness, if it can be called a weakness, was that he had realized his ambitions.   He had reached a position of supreme power, which he was not reluctant to abandon" (p. 170).   Bolívar's admirers will refute this statement as a gross simplification.

*Walton, Richard J.   The United States and Latin America.   (New York: The Seabury Press, 1972, 161 p.) Grades: 9-12.

From a very comprehensive and objective position, this book describes the difficult relationship that has existed between the United States and Latin America since the early 1800s until 1970.   Readers who are interested in a thorough explanation of the historical, political, and economic forces that have prevailed between the U.S. and Latin America will find this book to be fascinating reading.   It includes the following excellent chapters: The Beginning, Spain's Grip Weakens, The Monroe Doctrine, Asserting the Doctrine, the Dawn of Imperialism, Dollar Diplomacy, President Wilson Intervenes, The Years of the Good Neighbor, Latin America and the Cold War, The United States vs. Cuba, The Recent Past, The Future.

This is how the author explains past U.S. interference in Latin America: "...the United States intervened for the mixture of selfish and unselfish reasons that has usually characterized its Latin American policies.   It genuinely wanted to help the people of these impoverished lands (invariably by attempting to impose American standards) and it was looking out for its own interests even if (as in Vietnam decades later) they were not really threatened" (p. 77).

Webb, Robert N.   Simón Bolívar: The Liberator.   (New York: Franklin Watts, 1966, 12 p.)   Grades: 7-10.

The author briefly and concisely narrates well-known highlights in the life of the liberator of Venezuela, New Granada (Colombia), Ecuador, Peru, and the founder of the Republic of Bolivia. Bolívar's early life as a member of one of Caracas's oldest, wealthiest, and most aristocratic families is contrasted with his life as a true military genius and leader. In the last chapter the author describes the political situation, until 1964, of the countries that Bolívar liberated.

Whitney, Alex. Voices in the Wind (Central and South American Legends). (New York: David McKay Company, 1976, 57 p.) Grades: 2-Adult.

An outstanding collection of legends from six pre-Columbian civilizations. Each story is preceded by an introduction to each culture describing its achievements with a black-and-white photograph of the area in which each civilization flourished. Each legend is about four or five pages long, told in simple and interesting language. An excellent one is "The Hunter Who Wanted Air," a legend from Guyana, Surinam, French Guinea, and Brazil, which emphasizes that "honesty ... is the first step on the path to 'wisdom,'" (p. 37). This book is an excellent introduction to the Mayas of Yucatan, the Aztecs of Mexico, the Quiché Mayas of Guatemala, the Chibchas of Colombia and Panama; the Amerinds of Guyana, Surinam, and Brazil, and the Incas of Ecuador, Bolivia, and Peru.

*Williams, Byron. Continent in Turmoil: A Background Book on Latin America. (New York: Parents' Magazine Press, 1971, 247 p.) Grades: 9-12.

This is a very good introduction to Latin America that emphasizes the continent's economic problems. It discusses the geographical and physical features, the differences and similarities, the history of Latin American countries, a study in greater detail of Argentina and Brazil, and the abuse and exploitation practiced by some European countries and the United States. The

author sets the stage to explain Latin America's problems by stating: "Today the word most used and most
relevant to Latin America as a bloc is 'underdeveloped, '
which is a polite word for a nation's failure to produce
enough goods and services to adequately employ, feed,
clothe, house, educate, and care for the health of its
people.   The word describes the economy of every
Latin American nation today" (pp. 11-12).   And, again:
"Children are still sold in some Latin American countries in the hope that as servants or as laborers--even
as prostitutes--they will be able to eat and live" (p. 19).
        The author describes the United States' role in
dominating the economies of Latin American countries
and quotes Josué de Castro regarding the huge profits
American companies make in Latin America: ". . . de-
pending on the case, United States profits in Latin
America are from fifty to two hundred percent higher
than those made in the United States. . . " (p. 122).
        Some of the facts in this book are now outdated,
but it is still a good background to the sad state of
Latin America.

Young, Bob and Jan.   Liberators of Latin America.
(New York: Lothrop, Lee & Shepard Co. , 1970, 218
p.)   Grades: 7-10.

        Brief biographies of nine heroes of Latin Amer-
ica that are written in an easy-to-understand manner.
They are: Toussaint L'Ouverture (Haiti), José de San
Martín (Argentina), Simón Bolívar (Venezuela), Dom
Pedro I (Brazil), Miguel Hidalgo, José Morelos, Agustín Iturbide and Benito Juárez (Mexico), and José
Martí (Cuba).   The authors' simple style might be appealing to young readers who have not been exposed to
Latin American heroes who fought for the independence
of their own countries.   One Spanish word is misspelled
repeatedly in the narrative: "gapuchines" [sic].

BOOKS REVIEWED IN THIS CHAPTER:

Bailey, Bernadine.   Famous Latin-American Liberators.
   Illus.:   Gerald McCann.   (New York: Dodd, Mead
   & Company, 1960, 153 p.)   Grades: 7-9.

Baker, Nina Brown.   He Wouldn't Be King: The Story
   of Simón Bolívar.   Illus.:   Camilo Egas.   (New
   York: The Vanguard Press, 1941, 300 p.)   Grades:
   7-12.

Baum, Patricia.   Dictators of Latin America.   (New
   York: G. P. Putnam's Sons, 1972, 186 p.)   Grades:
   6-12.

Borreson, Mary Jo.   Let's Go to South America.   Illus.:   Jane Evans.   (New York: G. P. Putnam's
   Sons, 1969, 45 p.)   Grades: 3-6.

Carter, William E.   The First Book of South America.
   Rev. ed. (New York: Franklin Watts, 1972, 86 p.)
   Grades: 4-6.

*Fisher, John R.   Latin America from Conquest to In-
   dependence.   (New York: The John Day Company,
   1971, 125 p.)   Grades: 9-12.

Goetz, Delia.   Neighbors to the South.   (New York:
   Harcourt, Brace & World, 1956, 163 p.)   Grades:
   7-9.

Joy, Charles R.   Getting to Know the River Amazon.
   Illus.:   Nathan Goldstein.   (New York: Coward-Mc-
   Cann, 1963, 61 p.)   Grades: 3-5.

May, Charles Paul.   Peru, Bolivia, Ecuador: The Indian Andes.   (New Jersey: Thomas Nelson, 1969,
   211 p.)   Grades: 7-12.

Nevins, Albert J.   Away to the Lands of the Andes.
   (New York: Dodd, Mead & Company, 1962, 95 p.)
   Grades: 5-8.

*Perry, Roger.   Patagonia: Windswept Land of the
South.   (New York: Dodd, Mead & Company, 1974,
117 p.)   Grades: 6-12.

*Prago, Albert.   The Revolutions in Spanish America:
The Independence Movements of 1808-1825.   (New
York: The Macmillan Company, 1970, 226 p.)
Grades: 9-12.

*Prieto, Mariana.   Play It in Spanish.   Illus. :   Regina
and Haig Sherkerjian.   (New York: The John Day
Company, 1973, 43 p.)   Grades: K-2.

Quinn, Vernon.   Picture Map Geography of Mexico, Central America, and the West Indies.   Illus. :   Da Osimo.   (New York: J. B. Lippincott Company, 1943
[revised 1963], 114 p.)   Grades: 4-6.

*Rink, Paul.   Soldier of the Andes: José de San Martín.
(New York: Julian Messner, 1971, 182 p.)   Grades:
7-12.

*Selsam, Millicent E. , editor.   Stars, Mosquitoes and
Crocodiles: The American Travels of Alexander Von
Humboldt.   Illus. :   Russell Francis Peterson.   (New
York: Harper & Row, 1962, 166 p.)   Grades: 7-12.

Syme, Ronald.   Bolívar: The Liberator.   Illus. :   William Stobbs.   (New York: William Morrow and Company, 1968, 190 p.)   Grades: 5-9.

*Walton, Richard J.   The United States and Latin Amer-
ica.   (New York: The Seabury Press, 1972, 161 p.)
Grades: 9-12.

Webb, Robert N.   Simón Bolívar: The Liberator.
(New York: Franklin Watts, 1977, 129 p.)   Grades:
7-10.

Whitney, Alex.   Voices in the Wind (Central and South
American Legends).   (New York: David McKay Company, 1976, 57 p.)   Grades: 2-Adult.

*Williams, Byron.   Continent in Turmoil: A Background
   Book on Latin America.   (New York: Parents' Magazine Press, 1971, 247 p.)   Grades: 9-12.

Young, Bob and Jan.   Liberators of Latin America.
   (New York: Lothrop, Lee & Shephard Co. , 1970,
   218 p.)   Grades: 7-10.

ARGENTINA

Argentina is the second-largest country in the
Southern Hemisphere, after Brazil.   It has some of the
richest topsoil in the world.   The pampas are cultivated
extensively in wheat, corn, grain, sorghum, and sun-
flower seed and provide year-round pasturage for many
of Argentina's beef cattle.   Argentina is one of the
world's chief exporters of food and agricultural products.
It exports wheat, fruit, fresh meat, and other animal
products, such as wool hides and canned and preserved
meats.   Because Argentina is south of the equator, the
seasons are reversed from those of the Northern Hemisphere.   When it snows in New York, it is summer in
Buenos Aires, and conversely, when it is summer in
New York it is winter in Buenos Aires.

More than one-third of Argentina's population is
centered in and around Buenos Aires, the largest metro-
politan area in South America and among the ten largest
cities in the world.   Most Argentines are of Spanish and
Italian descent, as the original Indian population, which
was mainly composed of hunting tribes, was eliminated
in the wars with the Argentine settlers.   Today there
are few mestizos or Indian groups.   The literacy rate
is one of the highest in Latin America and about one-
half of the people may be considered middle class.
Even though 72 percent of Argentina's residents live in
urban areas, the gaucho, like the American cowboy, is
a central figure in folk literature and music.   The
gaucho today is an estancia employee and does work
similar to that of the American cowboy.

The following are nonfiction and fiction books that introduce students to Argentina and its people.   (Asterisks indicate noteworthy books.)

Caldwell, John C.   Let's Visit Argentina.   (New York: The John Day Company, 1961, 95 p.)   Grades: 3-6.

The author intended to write for boys and girls in the United States about boys and girls in Argentina. He explains that in Argentina they "...may speak a different language; soccer, rather than baseball, may be the national game; summer vacation comes in December and January rather than in the summer; but still we are much alike....   The history of our countries is much alike.   Our ancestors fought for independence as did the Argentines of the same period" (p. 95).   This book has a serious flaw, it is greatly outdated.   For example, the following applies to Argentina in the 1950s: "On the streets are thousands of very old-model automobiles. Many cars have been driven so long that their owners can hardly keep the pieces together" (p. 31), and, "Instead of using trucks, the milkmen travel their routes in horse-drawn wagons" (p. 33).   The author believes that young readers should learn about Argentina because, "The communists would like to stir up trouble.   They would like Latin Americans to become discontented with their present life and then become communist.   They try to make people hate and fear the United States" (p. 12).

Carpenter, Allan.   Enchantment of Argentina.   (Chicago: Children's Press, 1969, 89 p.)   Grades: 5-9.

Argentina's geography, history, economy, government, people (among them the gauchos), and natural resources are described in a very clear, direct style.   Of special interest to young readers should be the chapter "Five Children of Argentina" (p. 10), in which the author wrote about five children who live in different parts of the country and who belong to different families: from the very wealthy family to a modest mestizo family.   The

reader should note that this book describes Argentina
up to 1968; some of the information is no longer true:
such as, Buenos Aires is "the largest Spanish city in
the world" (p. 80). Nonetheless, the attractive photographs and maps in color and black-and-white and the
informative view of Argentina make this book a useful
introduction to the country.

Ellis, Ella Thorp. Roam the Wild Country. (New
York: Atheneum, 1967, 209 p.) Grades: 4-6.

    Through Martin, a thirteen-year-old from Argen-
tina, the reader is exposed to the adventurous life of
Argentina's gauchos. This book includes all the excitement of living and working on a large "Estancia":
breaking wild horses, searching for water during the
worst drought in fifty years, surviving a storm while
protecting a large herd of horses, killing a puma, fighting a stranger, plunging a knife into a horse to suck out
the venom of a poisonous snake, as well as the satisfac-
tions of becoming a gaucho.

*Hall, Elvajean. The Land and People of Argentina.
Rev. ed. (New York: J. B. Lippincott Company, 1972,
155 p.) Grades: 6-10.

    This is an interesting introduction to Argentina,
its history, and its people. The author offers simple
contrasts to explain differences between the United States
and Argentina: "[In North America] we had settlers; in
South America they had exploiters ... the exploiters
might have been called FERDINAND AND COLUMBUS,
INCORPORATED.... Everything done in the New World
had to meet one test only: would it make money for the
crown?" (p. 45). The author then continues to explain
that no trade could be shipped through the port of Buenos
Aires during Spanish Colonial times. It describes Argentina's fight for independence; Juan Domingo Perón,
and his controversial wife Eva Duarte; the gauchos;
and life in Buenos Aires: "One of the first things a
visitor today notices is the appearance of wealth and

luxury.... The fashionable shopping streets, Avenida
Santa Fe and calle Florida, can be compared with Fifth
Avenue in New York" (p. 109). And, also true:
"... Argentina is the one South American country in which
there is a large middle class" (p. 117).

Hornos, Axel. Argentina, Paraguay, & Uruguay. (New
Jersey: Thomas Nelson, 1969, 218 p.) Grades: 6-10.

It is indeed interesting to read an Argentine's
view of Argentina, Paraguay, and Uruguay. But young
readers may wonder why the author chose to begin his
book with a description of the life of very primitive Indians, who "still lead lives not far removed from the
Dark Ages" (p. 20). The author presents a positive
view of the role of the Catholic Church in the New
World. Regarding the Spanish Conquest, he states that
its purpose was "to convert and civilize, even at the
cost of the most extraordinary hardships, so that the
natives might share the blessings of Christian faith and
Spanish culture" (p. 34). Some of the chapters are too
wordy, but there are interesting descriptions of young
people in Argentina, the Guaraní Indians of Paraguay,
and the tragedy of small towns in Argentina, where "too
often their youths drift aimlessly through life because,
once the school years are over, nothing is done on a
communal basis to stimulate their minds toward pursuits
more challenging than the mere struggle for survival"
(p. 115).

Kalnay, Francis. Chúcaro Wild Pony of the Pampa.
Illus.: Julian de Miskey. (New York: Harcourt, Brace
& World, 1958, 127 p.) Grades: 4-8.

As stated in the foreword: "This is the story of
some people who lived in the heart of the Argentine
Pampa--men, women, boys--of one boy especially, and
a horse, a very special horse" (p. 11). It includes descriptions of: "some mighty fine gauchos" (p. 17); "the
flat, boundless Pampa, where for miles and miles you
see nothing but grass" (p. 23); "a gaucho dinner" (p. 53);

and "a good-sized Argentine estancia, " which "is not like a farm.   It is much larger than that.   It is as big as fifty or a hundred farms joined together" (p. 60).

Through the affection of a young gaucho boy for his pony, the reader is exposed to the life of the gauchos and a wealthy plantation owner.

Olden, Sam.   Getting to Know Argentina.   Illus.:   Haris Petie.   (New York: Coward-McCann, 1961,   59 p.) Grades: 3-7.

In a simple, easy-to-understand narrative the reader is guided through Argentina: starting with a parade in downtown Buenos Aires the author tells about Argentina's heroes of the independence movement and the city's magnificent avenues, buildings, and shops: "In almost every block, you spy a newsstand or bookshop.   Argentines love to read--and 93 percent of them can.   A greater percentage of people can read and write in Argentina than in any other Latin American country" (p. 25), with an appropriate illustration; life of a middle-class family and their visit to the opera; a view of the country's lush pampas, jungle, Iguazú Falls, and a visit with gauchos in a great ranch.   Gauchos "are South America's cowboys, among the most superb horsemen of the world" (p. 50).   There are two commercials for Pan American jet clippers in the text, perhaps in appreciation "for the transportation that enabled the author to undertake the field research for this book" (Acknowledgments).

BOOKS REVIEWED IN THIS CHAPTER:

Caldwell, John C.   Let's Visit Argentina.   (New York: The John Day Company, 1961, 95 p.) Grades: 3-6.

Carpenter, Allan.   Enchantment of Argentina.   (Chicago: Children's Press, 1969, 89 p.) Grades: 5-9.

Ellis, Ella Thorp.   Roam the Wild Country.   (New York: Atheneum, 1967, 209 p.) Grades: 4-6.

✕ *Hall, Elvajean.　The Land and People of Argentina.
　　Rev. ed.　(New York:　J. B. Lippincott Com-
　　pany, 1972, 155 p.)　Grades:　6-10.

✕ Hornos, Axel.　Argentina, Paraguay, & Uruguay.
　　(New Jersey:　Thomas Nelson, 1969, 218 p.)
　　Grades:　6-10.

Kalnay, Francis.　Chúcaro Wild Pony of the Pampa.
　　Illus.:　Julian de Miskey.　(New York:　Harcourt,
　　Brace & World, 1958, 127 p.)　Grades:　4-8.

Olden, Sam.　Getting to Know Argentina.　Illus. :
　　Haris Petie.　(New York:　Coward-McCann, 1961,
　　59 p.)　Grades:　3-7.

CHILE

Chile is a long, narrow strip of mountainous land located on the extreme southwest coast of South America. Some of the world's highest mountain peaks and greatest ocean depths are within or near Chile's borders. Chile has three major geographical regions: the northern portion is desert and contains great mineral wealth, primarily copper and nitrates; the small central portion dominates the economy in terms of population and agricultural resources; and the southern portion is rich in forests and grazing lands and has a string of volcanoes and lakes.

Over 70 percent of Chile's population live in the largest cities, which are located in central Chile. The important cities are Santiago, the capital; Valparaíso, the principal port; Viña del Mar, the leading seaside resort; and Concepción, the third largest city in the nation, after Valparaíso. Most of the people are mestizo of Spanish-Indian ancestry; however, there are about 400,000 pure-blooded Indians, mostly descendants of the legendary Araucanians.

Chile has the largest copper deposit in the world. Copper is its chief product and export, despite fairly low copper prices in the world today. Iron ore is Chile's second-most-valuable mineral export. Chile also is Latin America's second largest wine producer.

The following nonfiction books will introduce students to Chile and its people. (Asterisks indicate noteworthy books.)

*Bowen, J. David.   The Land and People of Chile.
(New York: J. B. Lippincott Company, 1976, 155 p.)
Grades: 7-10.

    This is a simple introduction to Chile's geogra-
phy, history, government, economy, culture, and people, with information current as of 1976.   It emphasizes
the problems of Chile's severe isolation during colonial
times, as well as its dependence on copper.   It briefly
mentions the "Chilean election of 1970 [that] was the
most important that had taken place in Latin America
in modern times....   It was the first time voters had
been given a clear opportunity to choose or to reject
Marxist principles.   Salvador Allende became the 'com-
rade president' of Chile" (p. 150).   Equally succinctly,
it states that on "September 11, 1973, in a move that
many had expected for months, the Chilean army called
for Allende's resignation.   He refused and swore he
would die at his post....   The socialist experiment was
over" (p. 155).

Carpenter, Allan.   Enchantment of Chile.   (Chicago:
Children's Press, 1969, 90 p.)   Grades: 5-9.

    Chile's geography, people, history, economy,
natural resources, and cities are described in a direct,
simple style.   Attractive photographs and maps in color
and black-and-white add interest to the easy-to-read
text.   Of special interest to young readers should be the
chapter "Five Children of Chile, " in which the author
described the lives of five different families who live in
different parts of the country: a wealthy, aristocratic
family; a businessman's family; and a shepherd's family.
The reader should note that this book describes Chile
until 1968; therefore, no mention is made of recent
events that have occurred in Chile after President Eduardo Frei's regime.

Chile in Pictures.   (New York: Sterling Publishing
Company, 1962, 64 p.)   Grades: 3-10.

    Although dated, this book includes many very
good black-and-white photographs of Chile: the land,

the history, the government, the people, and the economy until 1958.   It also contains many facts that are now outdated, such as population, "... Santiago is reputed to be the third most expensive city in the world" (p. 37).   This is certainly not true any more.   And the following is a strong assertion that should be questioned: "Though they lack the fiery spirit of their more Latin neighbors, some of the more exasperating aspects of Latin casualness are lacking too; in Chile, most business appointments are kept on time, buses, elevators, and heating systems function smoothly.   The influence of the German population seems to have given most Chileans a far more businesslike and efficient manner than we usually associate with Latin America" (p. 39).

Pendle, George.   The Land and People of Chile.   (New York: The Macmillan Company, 1960,   87 p.)   Grades: 6-10.

A very readable description of the geography, historical development, economics, and people of Chile narrated in a most personal style.   The British style of the author is apparent in many anecdotes that tell about well-known British authors who visited Chile in the eighteenth century and in excerpts from the journal of Maria Graham, a young Englishwoman, who in 1822 happened to be staying at a country cottage outside Valparaíso.   It introduces the reader to the origins of the nitrate industry in Chile, to the first railway, and to the importance of copper to Chile's economy.   The following is not a well-known fact: "One of the most prominent Communists is none other than Pablo Neruda, who was born in the rainy south in 1904 and is not only Chile's, but Latin America's, most famous living poet. Neruda has visited the U. S. S. R. and has written many rather tiresome verses in honour of that country..." (p. 70).   This is a very enjoyable introduction to Chile up to 1959.

BOOKS REVIEWED IN THIS CHAPTER:

*Bowen, J. David.   The Land and People of Chile.
  (New York: J. B. Lippincott Company, 1976,
  155 p.) Grades: 7-10.

Carpenter, Allan.   Enchantment of Chile.   (Chicago:
  Children's Press, 1969, 90 p.)   Grades: 5-9.

Chile in Pictures.   (New York: Sterling Publishing
  Company, 1962, 64 p.) Grades: 3-10.

Pendle, George.   The Land and People of Chile.
  (New York: The Macmillan Company, 1960, 87
  p.) Grades: 6-10.

COLOMBIA

Colombia, located in the northwest corner of South America, faces the Pacific Ocean and the Caribbean Sea. Its high western plateaus and valleys provide fertile soil where a variety of tropical and semitropical crops can be grown. Colombia has many forests and mountains, as well as a hot jungle that is still undeveloped.

Bogotá, the capital, is the cultural and commercial center of the country. To Bogotá come not only the political leaders of the country, but also its students, artists, and writers. Most of the country's museums and universities are located there, as well as newspapers and periodicals (which are distributed over the country by air). About 95 percent of the people are Roman Catholic. And, even though in recent years there has been some separation of church and state, the Catholic Church still retains some important powers, such as the right to give religious instruction in all public schools.

Coffee is the main support of Colombia's economy. Colombia is the world's second largest producer and exporter (after Brazil) of coffee. Colombian coffee is regarded by many as one of the world's best and normally receives a special price on the world market. Due to Colombia's diverse climate and topography, a great variety of crops can be grown. Cacao, sugarcane, coconuts, bananas, plantains, rice, tobacco, cassana, and most of the nation's cattle are produced in the hot regions. Coffee, corn, and other vegetables and fruits are grown in the temperate regions. The cold regions produce wheat, barley, potatoes, cold-climate vegetables, dairy cattle, and poultry.

The following fiction and nonfiction books will introduce students to Colombia and its people.   (Asterisks indicate noteworthy books.)

*Broderick, Walter J.   Camilo Torres: A Biography of the Priest-Guerrillero.   (New York: Doubleday and Company, 1975, 340 p.)   Grades: 10-Adult.

A well-written biography that describes the life and times of Camilo Torres, a modern priest-turned-guerrillero from a wealthy Colombian family, who was killed in 1966.   Torres's growing-up years in an elitist society in Bogotá, his education and final rebellion against the Roman Catholic Church, and his life and death as a member of a small guerrilla band in Colombia's jungles provide the reader with an interesting view of life in Colombia.   The author writes passionately against the oligarchy's abuse of power: "Camilo's was an accurate diagnosis; the oligarchy as usual had manipulated the situation to their advantage.   In order to halt the rising fury of the masses they had brought pressure to bear on the arrogant and pouting President Valencia....   In fact, in all its long experience of power, the Colombian oligarchy had known only one peril which it recognized as mortal: the armed insurrection of the peasants.   The oligarchs' most dramatic and repressive measures had always been employed to crush each peasant uprising... " (p. 218).

Caldwell, John C.   Let's Visit Colombia.   (New York: The John Day Company, 1962, 93 p.)   Grades: 3-7.

Basic facts about Colombia are interspersed with general information about the Spanish language and the Latin American customs of taking the father's and mother's last names.   The strong role of the Catholic Church is emphasized: "According to the constitution, there is freedom of worship in Colombia.   However, the

Catholic Church holds such an important position that it
can and sometimes does discourage worship in Protestant churches.   There has been some persecution of
people who are not Catholics" (p. 74).

Unfortunately the author added his own interpretation of bullfights without attempting to understand them:
"As we have said, bullfighting is dangerous.   Matadors
are sometimes injured or even killed.   It is a bloody
sport, and many North Americans do not care to watch
the bullfight" (p. 82).   And the author's strong feelings
impelled him to write seven pages against communism:
"Perhaps even more important, the Communist leaders
of Cuba are now trying to spread Communism throughout Central and South America.   Communist agents go
from Cuba to neighboring countries trying to turn all of
Latin America against the United States" (p. 88).

Carpenter, Allan, and Jean Currens Lyon.   Enchantment of Colombia.   (Chicago: Children's Press, 1969,
89 p.)   Grades: 5-8.

Attractive photographs and maps and simple text
describe Colombia's geography, history, people, natural
resources, economy, and important cities up to 1966.
Of special interest to young readers should be the section on Agriculture (pp. 64-70), which explains why the
"coffee industry is the mainstay of the Colombia economy, " and the chapter "Four Children of Colombia, "
which tells about the life of an Indian girl, who lives
in the Colombian Andes; a mulatto boy, who lives in the
city of Santa María; a Ticuna Indian boy, who lives
deep in the jungle close to the Amazon River; and a
wealthy boy from Bogotá, whose family has owned a
coffee plantation for several generations.

*Landry, Lionel.   The Land and People of Colombia.
(New York: J. B. Lippincott Company, 1970, 154 p.)
Grades: 7-12.

A very well written description of the land and
people of Colombia that enthusiastically tells about its

history, geography, cities, religion, agriculture, economy, and arts until 1969.   The author is very optimistic about Colombia's future and seems to be a true
admirer of the country.   Nevertheless, he tries to give
a balanced view of Colombia's problems: "To understand Colombia today, one cannot go on thinking in
terms of a small, all-powerful oligarchy and a huge
horde of persecuted peasants rising in anger against it.
The real situation is more complicated and more hopeful" (p. 60).

The author repeatedly emphasizes what he believes is a big difference between Colombia and other
Latin American countries: "The huge haciendas of
nearby nations are not, with only a very few (and dim-
inishing) exceptions, to be found in Colombia. ...   Colombia is thus a rather startling exception to the myth of
the Latin American oligarchy" (p. 61).

Van Iterson, S. R.   The Curse of Laguna Grande.
(New York: William Morrow and Company, 1973, 190
p.)   Grades: 7-9.

An absorbing mystery story set around Laguna
Grande, an isolated lake in Colombia.   The extreme
contrasts between the wealthy "hacendados" and the
superstitious, ignorant people are depicted through Carlos Arturo, the young hero, who gradually uncovers the
reasons for his father's disappearance, and the country
people, whose only source of knowledge is a woman
thought to have magical powers.   The author presents
a very negative picture of the country people: "... it
was not in the nature of these country people to speak
plainly.   They were always devious, especially when ill
at ease or afraid" (p. 95).   A good mystery story that
unfortunately presents a very superficial view of Colombia.

Van Iterson, S. R.   Village of Outcasts.   (New York:
William Morrow and Company, 1972, 190 p.)   Grades:
7-9.

A very well written mystery story that includes jealousy, revenge, and murder in a leper colony in a small village in Colombia.   The problems of rejection experienced by all the sick people as well as the intrigues in the village make this a particularly depressing story.   Through Pilar, the reader is exposed to the life of a strange, wealthy Colombian family, and through Claudio, the teenage hero, the reader experiences the limited opportunities that many village people have in Colombia.

BOOKS REVIEWED IN THIS CHAPTER:

*Broderick, Walter J.   Camilo Torres: A Biography of the Priest-Guerrillero.   (New York: Doubleday and Company, 1975, 340 p.)   Grades: 10-adult.

Caldwell, John C.   Let's Visit Colombia.   (New York: The John Day Company, 1962, 93 p.)   Grades: 3-7.

Carpenter, Allan, and Jean Currens Lyon.   Enchantment of Colombia.   (Chicago: Children's Press, 1969, 89 p.)   Grades: 5-8.

*Landry, Lionel.   The Land and People of Colombia. (New York: J. B. Lippincott Company, 1970, 154 p.)   Grades: 7-12.

Van Iterson, S. R.   The Curse of Laguna Grande. (New York: William Morrow and Company, 1973, 190 p.)   Grades: 7-9.

Van Iterson, S. R.   Village of Outcasts.   (New York: William Morrow and Company, 1972, 190 p.)   Grades: 7-9.

CUBA

Cuba, the largest island in the West Indies, lies on the northern boundary of the Caribbean Sea ninety-two miles south of Key West, Florida. It is a beautiful island about the size of Pennsylvania, with a mild, tropical climate and vegetation. The capital, Havana, located on the northwest coast, is the principal port and city.

Cuba was a Spanish colony for 388 years. During Spanish colonial times, the settlers devoted themselves mainly to growing sugarcane and tobacco. As the native Indian population died out, slaves were brought from Africa to work on the plantations. The population of Cuba is now composed largely of people of Spanish and African origins. It is estimated that 51 percent of the people are mulatto, 37 percent are white, 11 percent are Negro, and 1 percent are Chinese. The adult literacy rate is now 96 percent.

Cuba's economy is heavily dependent upon sugar, which accounts for a great majority of its export earnings. For this reason, Cuba's economic growth is primarily a function of the world price of sugar. Cuba has among the world's largest reserves of nickel, and this together with tobacco and sugar constitute the main exports. Cuba must import capital goods, industrial raw materials, food, and petroleum.

The Communist Party is Cuba's only legal political party. Fidel Castro is First Secretary of the party and his brother Raul is Second Secretary. Fidel

Castro is also Commander-in-Chief of the Armed
Forces.   Cuba receives strong economic assistance
from the Soviet Union, which comes primarily in the
form of balance-of-payments support and subsidy payments for sugar and nickel from Cuba and petroleum
shipments into Cuba.

In the early 1960s many middle-class technicians,
managers, and white-collar workers fled from Cuba to
the United States.   Many settled in Miami, Florida, and
other cities in the United States.

The following fiction and nonfiction books describe
Cuba and its people from several perspectives.   Readers should note that Fidel Castro has aroused the emotions of many authors with quite different points of view.
(Asterisks indicate noteworthy books.)

Baum, Patricia. Cuba: Continuing Crisis.   (New
York: G. P. Putnam's Sons, 1971, 152 p.)
Grades: 6-9.
It would be very sad indeed to expose young
readers to Cuba and its problems through this rambling
indictment of the horrible evilness of Communism and
this emotional denunciation of Fidel Castro, who is described as "a mere pawn of the Soviet Union--and an
expendable pawn" (p. 140) and "as a powerless puppet"
(p. 141).   From Chapter 1, "Cuba Today, " the author
begins her endless reproaches of Castro's regime:
"... Castro wants every Cuban to learn at firsthand,
from aching backs and sweaty brows, that farm labor
is the base of his island-nation's economy..." (p. 10).
"Nearly everything in Cuba is in short supply and ra-
tioned" (p. 12).   "... Cuba has become an unbearable
place to live, and they [the Cubans] despair of hearing
Castro's perpetual promises of a brighter future" (p.
17).   This book includes five chapters that give a brief
survey of Cuba's history and five that describe Castro's
Cuba as a dictatorship with an endless "agony of tyranny
and poverty. "

Bishop, Curtis.   Little League Amigo.   (Philadelphia:
J. B. Lippincott Company, 1964, 187 p.)   Grades: 4-6.

      Through Carlos Galvez and his father the reader
is introduced to a wealthy Cuban family that had "to
escape from the Castro regime. "   Carlos is invited to
play Little League baseball, and develops very good
friendships with the American boys on the team.   Several misunderstandings occur that disturb Carlos, a
highly educated boy, and his American friends.   The
author explains these as cultural differences: Carlos's
readiness to talk openly about his baseball ability is re-
sented by some of the boys on the team.   Carlos explains to them, "My people are completely honest with
themselves as with everyone else.   We do not pretend
virtues we do not possess" (p. 37).   Carlos's formal
manners are also contrasted with the American boys'
informality.   Carlos finds this informality difficult to
adjust to.   And, when Carlos disagrees with the team's
manager, Carlos's father explains that Cuban people "are
sincere and well meaning, but too often we are impulsive
and self-centered.   We find it difficult to accept discip-
line of any sort.   Our conception of freedom is too
much of a narrow personal concept.   We aspire to complete individuality without responsibility" (p. 112).
Fast-moving baseball story in which cultures and friendships are questioned and explored.

Chadwick, Lee.   Cuba Today.   (Connecticut: Lawrence
Hill and Company, 1975, 212 p.)   Grades: 9-12.

      It is indeed amazing how one person can pretend
to know so much about one country and its people after
only "a three months' personal quest, " without even
knowing the language of the people.   Such is the case
of Chadwick, who narrates "a traveller's view of Cuba
with all 'the limitations' that implies" (p. 7).   Part I
is the background to the new Cuba: its history, guerilla
war, and from national liberation to socialism.   In
Part II the author examines "some of the effects of this
historic change, particularly on the lives of children and
young people" (p. 65) whom the author met on her brief

visit to Cuba.   The author is to be commended for conveying her enthusiasm about the achievements of Cuba's
revolution; however, the reader must be reminded that
these are the personal impressions of a well-intentioned
tourist.   Her reactions many times reflect a most positive, optimistic view of life: "As was often the case
while I was in Cuba, I found the absence of strain that
comes from individual competition which here is re-
placed by a sense of belonging to a group by whom you
as an individual are needed and to whose progress you
contribute by developing your capabilities" (p. 75-76).
Hopefully, the Cuban people today feel as cheerful about
their future as this author seems to believe they do.

Cowan, Rachel. Growing Up Yanqui. (New York: The
Viking Press, 1975, 142 p.)   Grades: 7-12.

     The author recounts her experiences as a young
teenager growing up in an upper-middle-class, white
Protestant, suburban community; as a disgruntled Peace
Corps trainee in Mexico; as a Peace Corps worker in
Ecuador; and as a tourist in Cuba.   Cowan is a very
good writer who expresses her ideas directly and succinctly; unfortunately her experiences in Latin America
are much too brief, and her lack of knowledge of economics limits her understanding of very complex factors
that cannot be solved as easily as she sometimes sug-
gests.   She describes very well Latin America's impoverished communities, whose people continue "to live
in one-room houses, eating beans and tortillas and wor-
rying about their sick children and their next day's
food" (p. 56), and she is honest in expressing her ad-
miration of the accomplishments of Castro's revolution,
as well as in questioning some of its results.   The author feels an "urgency to do something about U. S.
policy toward Latin America... we must stop sending
troops and C. I. A. agents to Latin America.   We must
cut off military aid to right-wing dictatorships and increase economic aid to governments that are pledged to
use it for programs that will serve all the people, not
just the oligarchs" (p. 139).

*Goldston, Robert. The Cuban Revolution. Illus.: Donald Carrick. (New York: The Bobbs-Merrill Company, 1970, 174 p.) Grades: 9-12.

A very readable and informative book that explains and analyzes the Cuban Revolution. It covers the early history of Cuba; the United States' involvements in Cuba in the 1900s which include the "infamous Platt Amendment... [which] declared that control of Cuba would be turned over to Cubans only after American interests had been secured... the Platt Amendment was to become a running sore in Cuban-American relations and a hateful symbol of Yankee domination... " (p. 46-47); the dismal conditions of life in Cuba before Castro's Revolution; why Castro's victory over Batista is only the first step toward a Cuban revolution: "... it would have to mean that real power--political, social and economic--had been transferred from the hands of the upper-middle-class owners of factories, casinos, sugar mills, plantations, businesses and utilities and their military-political governing apparatus into the hands of Cuba's workers and peasants... " (p. 111-112); and the outstanding accomplishments of the Castro regime in Cuba until 1965. Regarding the U.S. role in Cuban affairs in 1960, the author emphasizes Cuba's achievements in education, reducing the cost of living, and redistribution of land to the landless. He states: "Independent surveys made by American individuals and groups in the spring of 1960 reported that more than 80% of the Cuban people supported their government enthusiastically and were especially devoted to Fidel Castro. This was the government that the United States was now secretly preparing to destroy" (p. 141).

*Haverstock, Nathan A., and John P. Hoover. Cuba in Pictures. (New York: Sterling Publishing Company, 1974, 63 p.) Grades: 6-12.

This is a very objective and well written book on Cuba. Black-and-white photographs add valuable information on the land, history, government, people, and economy of Cuba. The authors have to be commended

for constantly keeping a balanced perspective on the
Castro regime: "The controversy over the pros and
cons of the Castro regime has been marked with an
emotionalism which has obscured the problems of the
Cuban people" (p. 5). The U. S. role in Cuban affairs
since 1898 is also objectively presented: "... the U. S.
military authorities did all of those things that would in
their eyes make occupied Cuba conform to the American
rather than the Cuban scale of cultural, social, and
political values. The result was that Cuba became a
client state--a protectorate--of the United States" (p.
28). It mentions many of the accomplishments of the
Castro government, as well as many of the incalculable
losses.

*Matthews, Herbert L. Cuba. (New York: The Mac-
millan Company, 1964, 129 p.) Grades: 9-12.

     This is a very good introduction to Cuba and the
early years of Fidel Castro's regime, with information
until 1964. It includes chapters on the island, the people, the way of life, the economy, independence, the
Republic, and the Revolution. It is a strong indictment
of the Spanish colonial period in Cuba: "The Spanish
ruled, often harshly and always to squeeze from the
island and its people every ounce of strength, every
pound of produce, and every bit of money that they
could" (p. 1).
     This book is slightly dated, as it emphasizes the
results of the Cuban Revolution up to 1964, such as
"... Americans cannot go there now and we do not know
what the cities will look like after the Revolution" (p.
13). But the interesting information that it includes
makes it very worthwhile. About the people, it states:
"The mixture in Cuba is white and black--Spanish and
African--... " (p. 18); "... at least one-quarter and perhaps as many as one-third of the Cubans are Negroes
or have Negro blood" (p. 22). It compares national
characteristics among the U. S. and Latin America in a
very realistic and easy-to-understand manner. And, in
an excellent chapter on Cuba's economy, it begins:
"Cuba was rightly called 'the world's sugar bowl. ' For
generations, one-quarter to one-third of the world's total
production of sugar was grown in Cuba" (p. 49).

Ortiz, Victoria.   The Land and People of Cuba.   (New
York: J. B. Lippincott Company, 1973, 152 p.)
Grades: 7-12.

        This is an interesting book, especially as a mar-
velous contrast to many books about Cuba that are highly critical of the Castro regime.   It begins with the history of Cuba from its discovery in the fifteenth century
to the results of the Castro government up through 1973.
In several instances it condemns the United States' influence in Cuba.   Regarding racial problems in Cuba,
it states: "With the increased influence of the United
States after 1902, and Cuba's development as the play-
land of wealthy North Americans, racial segregation
became a harsh fact, if not a legal one" (p. 39).   And,
shortly after this statement, it praises the new government: "It has been only since 1959 that Cuba has
moved rapidly toward becoming a truly open society
from a racial or ethnic point of view" (p. 39).   Regarding the Cubans who fled Castro's Cuba, it states:
"... many who have come to feel that their flight from
Cuba was perhaps precipitous.   They have heard from
relatives that things are not as bad as they had feared,
that in fact in many ways things are a great deal better
in Cuba than they had thought" (p. 105).   The message
of this book is that "there is no denying that in purely
human terms life is immeasurably better for the average
Cuban today than it was prior to 1959" (p. 149).   The
author argues intelligently for Castro's successes in
Cuba; but can one be so sure after only "visiting Cuba
during the summer of 1963"?

Prieto, Mariana.   Johnny Lost.   Illus.:   Catherine
Hanley.   (New York: The John Day Company, 1969,
46 p.)   Grades: 2-4.

        Johnny, a seven-year-old Cuban boy, is always
getting lost.   This story centers around Johnny's lost-
and-found adventures at the Miami Airport and at the
police station.   The generosity shown to this Cuban
family by the Freedom House (an H. E. W. office), as
well as the kindness of "all these wonderful people.

Their color or size or nationality made no difference"
(p. 45), may be marvelous things, but they do not
make for an enjoyable story.   The text is in English
and Spanish, which could potentially attract more readers.   The illustrations are as stilted as the story.

*Williams, Byron.   Cuba: The Continuing Revolution.
(New York: Parents' Magazine Press, 1969, 216 p.)
Grades: 9-12.

        In the introduction to this book José Keselman
of Columbia University states that the author "has ex-
hibited an honesty toward Cuba that is all too rare in
our history books.   It is impossible to write an honest
book about Cuba without destroying the image of the
United States government as faultless, humane, chari-
table, and selfless.   Mr. Williams has been forthrightly
truthful, and he is to be particularly commended" (p.
9).   Even though it is indeed difficult to write about
Cuba, especially about recent developments there, from
a completely objective perspective, this author has certainly tried to narrate as many sides as possible of
Cuba's history.   This book includes Cuba's discovery
in 1492, its early struggles, revolution, U. S. interven-
tion, Castro's changes, and contemporary Cuba until
1968.   The author's intentions in reporting an unbiased
view of Cuba may be best exemplified by his evaluation
of Castro's revolution: "Clearly, life in the revolution
had its hardships and inconveniences.   For many, those
hardships proved intolerable, and they left Cuba, either
to take up arms against the revolution or simply to find
a more congenial life elsewhere.   Most Cubans, however, supported the revolution with varying degrees of
enthusiasm in spite of the claims that it made on them,
in spite of the danger from its enemies in which it
placed them, and in spite of the very new ways of living
that it demanded of them" (p.   213).

BOOKS REVIEWED IN THIS CHAPTER:

Baum, Patricia.   Cuba: Continuing Crisis.   (New York:
    G. P. Putnam's Sons, 1971, 152 p.)   Grades: 6-9.

Bishop, Curtis. Little League Amigo. (Philadelphia: J. B. Lippincott Company, 1964, 187 p.) Grades: 4-6.

Chadwick, Lee. Cuba Today. (Connecticut: Lawrence Hill and Company, 1975, 212 p.) Grades: 9-12.

Cowan, Rachel. Growing Up Yanqui. (New York: The Viking Press, 1975, 142 p.) Grades: 7-12.

*Goldston, Robert. The Cuban Revolution. Illus. : Donald Carrick. (New York: The Bobbs-Merrill Company, 1970, 174 p.) Grades: 9-12.

*Haverstock, Nathan A. , and John P. Hoover. Cuba in Pictures. (New York: Sterling Publishing Company, 1974, 63 p.) Grades: 6-12.

*Matthews, Herbert L. Cuba. (New York: The Macmillan Company, 1964, 129 p.) Grades: 9-12.

Ortiz, Victoria. The Land and People of Cuba. (New York: J. B. Lippincott Company, 1973, 152 p.) Grades: 7-12.

Prieto, Mariana. Johnny Lost. Illus. : Catherine Hanley. (New York: The John Day Company, 1969, 46 p.) Grades: 2-4.

*Williams, Byron. Cuba: The Continuing Revolution. (New York: Parents' Magazine Press, 1969, 216 p.) Grades: 9-12.

MEXICO

Mexico is the most populous Spanish-speaking country in the world. It shares a border with California, Arizona, New Mexico, and Texas. Mexico's topography ranges from low desert plains and jungle-like coastal strips to high plateaus and rugged mountains.

The people of Mexico are very proud of their pre-Columbian and Spanish heritage. Some of the major pre-Columbian cultures were the Olmec, Maya, Toltec, Aztec, and Mixtec-Zapotec. Their high level of civilization was evident in their architecture, arts, scientific accomplishments, and educational and governmental organizations. Spain's influence may still be seen through the language, religion, family life, customs, social life, and architecture. Today Mexican people maintain many of the arts, handicrafts, fiestas, and customs from their Indian and Spanish ancestors and blend them with their modern life, creating a unique culture.

More than half of the people live in central Mexico, where Mexico City is also situated. There is a constantly increasing migration from the rural areas to the cities. Mexico City, one of the largest cities in the world, now has a population of thirteen million people. Like other big cities it has many advantages and disadvantages--nice restaurants, theaters, museums, fine stores, and business opportunities--as well as problems in traffic, air pollution, noise, and housing.

Mexico is rich in mineral resources, and there is great hope that the recent discovery of extensive new oil fields will assist the country in its economic develop-

ment.   Much work needs to be done to solve Mexico's
many economic and social problems.

Mexican and Mexican-American people have lived
in the southwestern part of the United States for many
centuries.   Their influence and contributions are felt in
many aspects of the life, language, food, and architecture of the Southwest and in cities elsewhere in the
United States.   Mexican-Americans have a unique blend
of Hispanic and American customs and lifestyles.

Due to the lack of employment opportunities in
Mexico, there is a large illegal ("undocumented") migration of Mexican workers into the United States.   The
United States and Mexico are now cooperating in their
efforts to solve this problem.

The following books describe Mexico and the
Mexican and Mexican-American people from many points
of view.   (For a more extensive list and discussions of
books on Mexican customs, lifestyles, heroes, folklore,
and history, see the author's A Bicultural Heritage
[Metuchen, N.J.:   The Scarecrow Press, Inc., 1978].)
(Asterisks indicate noteworthy books.)

Atwater, James D., and Ramón Eduardo Ruiz.   Out
From Under: Benito Juárez and the Struggle for Mexi-
can Independence.   Illus.:   Paul Hogarth.   (New York:
Doubleday and Company, 1969, 111 p.)   Grades: 6-12.

Even though this book pretends to be the story
of "Benito Juárez and the Struggle for Mexican Independence, " it really covers the history of Mexico from
the time of the Aztecs until today.   It describes the
Aztecs' practice of human sacrifice; Cortes's conquest
of Montezuma's empire; Spanish colonialism in the New
World; the French and American Revolutions' influence
in Mexico; Santa Anna's masterful schemes in abusing
power in Mexico; the conflict between Mexico and the
U.S.; Maximilian and Carlotta's tragic empire; and the
U.S. influence in forcing the French out of Mexico.
Interspersed with all of these important times in Mexi-

co's history, there are references to Benito Juárez's
personal and political life. I think that this book will
confuse most young readers who are unfamiliar with
Mexico's troubled past. Unappealing illustrations make
Mexico's history seem like a story of bandits and cowboys.

Baker, Betty. No Help at All. Illus.: Emily Arnold
McCully. (New York: Greenwillow Books, 1978, 56
p.) Grades: K-2.

Even though this story is supposed to be an
adaptation of a Mayan legend, it truly lacks the appeal
of a genuine Mayan legend or a simply told children's
story. A Mayan rain god expects help around his
house from a boy he saved from a man-eating thing.
But the boy is not much help to the god, and the god
sends him home. The illustrations are feeble approxi-
mations to the marvels of Mayan civilization.

Baker, Betty. Walk the World's Rim. (New York:
Harper & Row, 1965, 168 p.) Grades: 5-8.

Chakoh, a fourteen-year-old Avavare Indian boy
from the Texas hills who "could not remember any
comfortable length of time... when he had not been cold
and hungry, " and Esteban, a Negro slave, became very
attached to each other as they experienced adventure,
hunger, and many injustices at the hands of the Spanish
conquistadores. In their long journey to Mexico City
they meet Pimas and Cheyennes, and hear about the
fabulous "seven golden cities of Antilia, Cibola. " This
book is an attempt to describe the Spanish conquistadores in Mexico in the sixteenth century ("It is hard to
explain, but such things as turquoise and gold have a
strange effect upon the gentlest of Spaniards" [p. 73])
and the life of several Indians tribes. Unfortunately,
it does justice to neither group. It should be read as
a story of a fourteen-year-old boy in search of his own
future. But superficial characterizations and unreal
situations result in a melodramatic story that should not

substitute for a good historical novel of the sixteenth century.

*Baker, Nina Brown. Juárez, Hero of Mexico. Illus.: Marion Greenwood. (New York: The Vanguard Press, 1942, 308 p.) Grades: 7-12.

     Benito Juárez, Mexico's greatest statesman, is presented as a shepherd boy, student, successful attorney, governor, president, and a constant defender of Mexico's Constitution and the rights of the humble people. The author writes about Juárez's personal and political life in a most readable manner, and by exercising many artistic prerogatives she explains Juárez's important achievements in a very easy-to-understand way, such as The Ley (Law) Juárez, The Constitution of 1857, and Juárez's role during Maximilian's brief regime in Mexico. The author also offers many personal glimpses of Juárez's devoted relationship to his wife, Margarita Maza. The author should be reproved for two unfortunate and unnecessary generalizations about Mexico: Describing Oaxaca, the capital of the state of Oaxaca, she states: "Oaxaca, where every day, almost, was fiesta day, with music dancing in the crowded streets." (pp. 13-14). And, Uncle Bernardino was "a widower, so that no scolding wife disturbed his prolonged siesta" (p. 20).

Bannon, Laura. Manuela's Birthday. (Chicago: Albert Whitman, 1972, 30 p.) Grades: K-3.

     This story combines all the "curios" of Mexico in thirty pages with ridiculous illustrations: sombreros, barefooted Indians, burros, and Manuela "wrapped her long shawl about her head and shoulders. This shawl was called a rebozo" (unnumbered). Manuela, a little Mexican girl with black hair, wanted a "doll with blue eyes and yellow hair" which her friends give her for her birthday. And, so that Manuela can remember her special day, her artist friends painted Manuela's fifth birthday recuerdo: a picture of Manuela "holding the

beautiful doll with blue eyes and yellow hair, and there
was the little baby burro in the picture, too" (unnumbered); with the appropriate ludicrous illustration.

*Beck, Barbara L.   The First Book of the Aztecs.
Illus.:   Page Cary.   (New York: Franklin Watts, 1966,
67 p.) Grades: 4-6.

     Excellent pictures and an easy-to-understand
text depict the achievements and daily life of the Aztecs.   This book includes Mexico's early civilizations;
the forming of the Aztec nation; the Aztecs, "people of
the sun"; education and the social classes; war and religion; the achievements of the Aztecs; Tenochtitlan;
and the Spanish conquistadores.   The author must be
commended for describing the Aztec civilization very
simply and yet preserving the authenticity of Aztec history.
     Many of the outstanding pictures that complement
the text were taken from original Aztec codexes that
add interest and reality to Aztec culture.   There is,
however, one oversight on page 65:   Cortés spoke
Spanish, not English.

Caldwell, John C.   Let's Visit Mexico.   (New York:
The John Day Company, 1965, 95 p.) Grades: 3-7.

     The back of the title page states: "data in this
edition brought up to date, 1973" and, even though there
is a slight improvement from the 1965 version, there
are still many of the same superficial observations or
misinterpretations (see Schon, Isabel.   A Bicultural
Heritage.   Scarecrow Press, 1978, pp. 99-100).
     For example, in the section on the Aztecs, the
author emphasized their practice of human sacrifice
and barely mentioned many of their outstanding, positive
achievements: "The main god of the Aztecs demanded
human sacrifice and constant war.   Aztec boys were
trained to seek prisoners who could then be sacrificed
to their bloodthirsty god" (pp. 31-32).   And, "We have
mentioned that the tribe was warlike, that human sacri-

fices were demanded by the Aztec gods, or so the Aztecs believed. The Aztecs ruled numerous weaker
tribes, and tribute or human beings for sacrifice was
continually demanded from the other tribes" (p. 33).
This author sensationalizes what thrills him about
Mexico but he neglects to write the story of Mexico.
About Mexico's natural resources, he states that "Mexico is one of the richest nations in petroleum or oil.
Each year about 100, 000, 000 barrels of oil are taken
from Mexico's rich oil fields" (p. 83). This author
pretends to be more knowledgeable than Mexican authorities in this area.

Carr, Harriett H. The Mystery of the Aztec Idol.
(New York: The Macmillan Company, 1959, 193 p.)
Grades: 4-6.

     A well-told mystery story that includes many
"curios" and tourist attractions of Mexico City and its
surroundings, such as Chapultepec Park, downtown
Mexico City, the Pyramids, Xochimilco, Taxco, Day
of the Dead, Mexican Christmas celebrations, piñatas,
and others. The hero is, of course, Mike, a nice boy
from Pennsylvania who has an exciting adventure in a
"strange" country. Gradually he gets to know and understand his two new Mexican friends, but there are
the endless beggars and "strange" people: "'All over
Mexico City you see people like that, with little fruit
for sale or maybe some two or three pieces of silver....
Or kids begging. It doesn't seem right to me, especially when some of them are so snooty and superior!'"
(p. 25). The following words in Spanish are misspelled
or misused: "Zocola" [sic] (p. 26); "gloriatas" [sic]
(p. 26); "Quién está usted?" [sic] (p. 155); "Pipicito"
[sic] (p. 160).

Cox, William. Chicano Cruz. (New York: Bantam
Books, 1972, 216 p.) Grades: 6-12.

     Exciting baseball story that describes the per-
sonal lives of four young baseball players who want very

much to succeed in the professional ranks.   Mando
Cruz, a poor Chicano from California; Sandy Roosevelt,
a poor black from New Jersey; Jack Kelly, a white boy
whose father is a drunk and a failure and hates Chicanos; and Gilbert Samson Jones III, a rich boy who
wanted to play ball.   This is a good sports story that
certainly conveys the drama of winning and losing as
well as the loneliness of constant traveling and the support among team members.

However, the author's description of Chicanos is
much too superficial.   He incessantly writes about the
food: "Chicanos eat the hot stuff, cook with the oils"
(p. 2).   And even though Mando Cruz is supposed to be
proud of his heritage, the only reference to his background is about his father who "had come to California
from Mexico as a wetback and had gained citizenship
only after great troubles" (p. 6).

Dedera, Don, and Bob Robles.   Goodbye García Adiós.
(Flagstaff, Arizona: Northland Press, 1976, 117 p.)
Grades: 7-12.

Black-and-white photographs of the early 1900s
and a bilingual (English and Spanish) text briefly narrate the life of Jesús García, a young Mexican railroad
engineer who lost his life trying to save an entire community in Nacozari, Sonora.

The format of the book, as well as the English
and Spanish texts, is very appealing.   The photographs
add an interesting glimpse of life in a small Mexican
town at the turn of this century.   However, Jesús García's life and times are superficially recited.   The
reader is left with a feeling of having read a few jour-
nalistic reports of the sad life of a daring young man
who: "made a mistake, for which he subsequently
heroically atoned with his life ... but he had not had
training in the capacity of a conductor; he was simply
an engineer, and young at that" (p. 86).

Dunnahoo, Terry.   This is Espie Sanchez.   (New York:
E. P. Dutton & Co., 1976, 156 p.)   Grades: 4-7.

Thrilling adventure story that tells about a Mexican-American teenage girl who works as an Explorer
scout with the Los Angeles Police.   The author uses
the Mexican-American community in Los Angeles as
the background for describing Mexican customs during
Christmas, such as "las posadas, " "nacimientos, " and
Mexican food.   Terry Dunnahoo can certainly write exciting stories that involve violence, murder, and mis-
understood teenagers; unfortunately, this describes only
the worst part of Mexico or Mexican people: poverty
in Tijuana, wetbacks, and Mexican-Americans on welfare or unemployed.   Perhaps the author realizes this,
as there are a few brief explanations: "The only handi-
cap she had to overcome were the screwballs who
thought Mexicans were lazier and dumber than paddies"
(p. 76).   And, "Tijuana is not Mexico.   Mexico is
Guadalajara, Mexico City, the mountains" (p. 121).
Mexican-American teenage heroes learn to survive and
hope amid a harsh reality.

Dunnahoo, Terry.   Who Needs Espie Sanchez?   (New
York: E. P. Dutton & Co. , 1977, 138 p.)   Grades:
6-9.

Esperanza Sanchez, a likable Mexican-American
girl who lives in L.A. 's El Barrio, is succeeding in
her efforts to keep a C average in school and to continue as an Explorer scout.   This fast-paced story includes a tragic automobile accident in which a boy is
killed and Espie's girlfriend Denise is sent to a hospital.   Espie meets Allison, a wealthy girl who drives
a sportscar, wears beautiful clothes, and drinks too
much.   This is exciting reading for young people; unfortunately, references to Mexicans or Mexican-Americans are often derogatory: Espie's thoughts about her
Mexican father and mother are indeed sad: ". . . it beat
having your father desert you and hearing your mother
tell the cops she didn't want you" (p. 21).   Again, about
her mother: ". . . watching her mother booze herself up
until she passed out on the couch the way she did last
year" (p. 4).   And, "'It beats living with my mother
and her boyfriends'" (p. 41).   And this, from a typical

conversation explaining the behavior of two vulgar men:
"'They're wetbacks, just in from Mexico, and they're
full of macho stuff'" (p. 73).

Epstein, Sam and Beryl.   The First Book of Mexico.
(New York: Franklin Watts, 1967, 86 p.) Grades: 4-6.

This is a simple introduction to Mexico written
in an easy-to-understand manner.   Even though the
historical and general information about Mexico still
applies, young readers should be told that the facts in
this book were true only as of 1966.   It describes
Mexico's fiestas, geography, farms and farmers, early
people, Montezuma and Cortés, New Spain, and a look
at the future.   This book is worth revising.

Friskey, Margaret.   Welcome to Mexico.   Illus. :
Lois Axeman.   (Chicago: Children's Press, 1975, 48
p.) Grades: 2-5.

Regrettably, this book is not a good introduction
to Mexico.   Most of the photographs show Mexico in
the 1950s, or show foreign tourists visiting the common
sites, or show only the "curios" scenes of Mexico's
cities and towns.   This book covers all the popular and
well-known tourist-type attractions of Mexico, but
leaves out many of the genuine aspects of the country
and its people.   Mexico is not a country exclusively
for tourists.

Grace, Nancy.   Earrings for Celia.   Illus. :   Helen
Siegl.   (New York: Pantheon, 1963, 46 p.) Grades:
3-5.

An absurd story that tells about a very poor
boy, Mario, his mother, and his little sister, who lived
near a "tiny village of Little Stones" in southern Mexico.   One day Mario's mother does not return from the
market of San Cristóbal, where she went to sell corn
at the market.   Mario's life of extreme poverty is

further saddened by his mother's sudden disappearance.
However, everything happens for the best: his mother
had been hurt by the "people from the North, " who
gave her many presents. And, Mario "wanted to thank
the Madre Bonita for her great kindness in allowing his
mother to be run over by an automobile" (p. 46).
    According to this author, Mexicans must be ex-
tremely poor and stupid.

Hancock, Ralph. Mexico. (New York: The Macmillan
Company, 1964, 117 p.) Grades: 6-9.

    This book contains much outdated information
that either is no longer true, or only existed in the
mind of its author: "Of all Mexicans, perhaps the
most interesting you will find in this dramatic land is
the Indian.... He will be barefooted or will wear
simple sandals made of old automobile tires or cow-
hide" (pp. 5-6). Obviously, the author chose to illus-
trate this book with innumerable photographs of poverty-
stricken "Indians. " In the chapter on "Visiting Mexico"
there are the following ridiculous admonitions: "Never
'go native' by trying typical dishes in the poor peoples'
restaurants and market stands.... Ladies do not wear
shorts or pants on public streets in Mexico.... Leave
pulque (made from the sap of the maguey) to the Indians, who have iron stomachs" (pp. 15, 17).
    In the chapter "A Land of History" the author
exaggerates and sensationalizes the Aztecs' practice of
human sacrifice and then ridicules a Mexican peasant
when he reports the explosion of the volcano Paricutín:
"For a moment the frightened peon wondered if he had
plowed too deep. Had he disturbed the Devil. He took
off his sombrero and scratched his head. He tried to
put out the fire by kicking dirt over dirt.... The ter-
rified man turned, and ran to tell his priest" (p. 85).
    Surely Mexico should not be seen from this au-
thor's absurd perspective!

Herman, Vic. Juanito's Railroad in the Sky. Illus. :
Vic Herman. (New York: Golden Press, 1976, 61 p.)
Grades: 2-6.

    Miguel Alvarez, a train engineer, his son Juan-
ito, who wants to become a good trainman, and Con-
chos, a Tarahumaran boy, who lives in the high cliffs
of the Sierra Madre, are the main characters in a
ridiculous journey from Los Mochis to Chihuahua.
Typical village scenes, absurd scenes of animals and
Mexican people riding on top of a train, burros and
passengers pushing the train, a train that runs out of
firewood, and Juanito's heroic act in driving the train
by himself result in a mockery of Mexico and its people. The lengthy text with a few Spanish words is bor-
ing and affected. Even though the author felt compelled
to end his story with a much-needed explanation ("Today ... thousands of tourists ride the 402 miles over
the Sierra Madre in modern, streamlined, air-condi-
tioned, vista-domed Pullman coaches powered by diesel
engines, or in modern, self-powered Fiat cars" [p.
61]), the story remains an absurdity that hopefully will
not attract too many young readers.

*Hobart, Lois. Mexican Mural: The Story of Mexico,
Past and Present. (New York: Harcourt, Brace &
World, 1963, 211 p.) Grades: 9-12.

    This is an outstanding book that portrays Mexico
and all its extremes, its people and their way of life,
as well as a simply written history of pre-Columbian,
colonial, and revolutionary Mexico. The author emphasizes and explains very well important differences between the United States and Mexico (pp. 55-58). In the
chapter on modern Mexico she describes some disagree-
able aspects: "One of the most serious difficulties of
government, and in fact of all phases of Mexican life
is graft in the form of the mordida" (p. 85). The author's amazing sensitivity to Mexican culture is evident
in her description of bullfights: 'It is only fair to try
to look at the corrida (bullfight) with the eyes of a
Mexican and not with our prejudices.... A really superb corrida demands the utmost in courage, power,
and grace from animal and man and is altogether a
singular experience..." (pp. 141-144).
    The main weakness of this book is that it needs

updating in its economic and educational statistics; the
information is true up to 1963. One unfortunate mistake: many Mexicans will disagree with the author's
opinions of Benito Juárez. He certainly did not estab-
lish "the tradition that a government candidate should
win any election by devious means against opposing
candidates" (p. 79).

Jennings, Gary. The Rope in the Jungle. (New York:
J. B. Lippincott Company, 1976, 225 p.) Grades:
5-7.

In the early 1900s a young boy and a ropemaker
set out into the heart of a Mexican jungle in the state
of Chiapas to splice back together a mysterious rope.
The story includes lots of excitement and thrilling adventures with wild animals, strange natives, enigmatic
forces, a helpful witch doctor, and a beautiful brave
girl. Unfortunately, the author makes some absurd al-
legations: " 'I've got to go back and huddle with a pack
of coyotes--that's what we call lawyers down there--' "
(pp. 24-25). Not true! He also elaborates on several
unpleasant aspects of Mexico: "...he had never seen a
seaport 'city' so wretched and ugly as this Coatzacoal-
cos" (pp. 62-63). And, even though the author briefly
mentions the greatness of the Maya and the Aztecs,
the emphasis is on primitive Mexican natives: " 'I
noticed that there was an odd and springy give to that
bridge.... Are you sure these natives are not cannibals?... Son, this rope isn't vine or grass. It's
twisted intestines!' " (p. 127).

Kalnay, Francis. It Happened in Chichipica. Illus.:
Charles Robinson. (New York: Harcourt Brace Jovanovich, 1971, 127 p.) Grades: 4-6.

A well-written, fast-moving story about Chucho,
a Mexican boy who lives on a small Mexican rancho.
It includes action, suspense, and mystery involving
various interesting characters that live in the town: the
curandero, the baker, the teacher, the town's villain,

etc.   Unfortunately, it emphasizes the same old stereotypes about Mexican people: "Alarm clocks are so un-
Mexican!" (p. 19); "by nine o'clock they are ready for
a hearty breakfast, a kind of brunch with tortillas and
beans, called frijoles" (p. 35).   Describing their village: "Yet look around, right here and over there,
and you see dirt, misery, sickness, drunkenness, and
terrible fights with guns and machetes" (p. 58).

Kirtland, J. G.   One Day in Aztec Mexico.   Illus. :
Jerome Snyder.   (New York: Harcourt, Brace &
World, 1963, 38 p.) Grades: 4-6.

By using a few Nahuatl words, the author constructed a silly story with even sillier illustrations that
is supposed to tell about Aztec Mexico.   The story
ridicules Aztec writing and Aztec customs.   The following is a sample of an absurd conversation between two
Aztecs: "'...how are your wives?...   They, too, are
very well, thank you....   And how are your children?...
Five or six of them were not feeling very well this
morning ... but the other forty are just fine, thank
you" (p. 23).   There is a glossary at the end of the
story, but nowhere is it explained that these are Nahuatl
words.

*Kouzel, Daisy.   The Cuckoo's Reward.   El Premio del
Cuco.   Illus. :   Earl Thollander.   (New York: Doubleday and Company, 1977, 28 p.) Grades: K-3.

An attractive adaptation of a Mayan legend that
tells why the gray cuckoo lost its splendid feathers and
beautiful singing voice and why "the cuckoo lays her
eggs in the nests of other birds, who raise her children for her" (unnumbered).   Because the text is in
simple English and Spanish it could appeal to children
who speak either language.

*Larralde, Elsa.   The Land and People of Mexico.   (New
York: J. B. Lippincott Company, 1964, 158 p.)
Grades: 6-12.

This is a very good overview of the history of Mexico until 1964. Unfortunately, many of the statistics, such as population and exports of natural resources, are now obsolete, and there are facts that are no longer true: The author states that in Mexico City "a subway is out of the question; there is too much water underneath the surface" (p. 122). Mexico City does have a beautiful modern subway. But this book has excellent chapters on the history of Mexico-- Ancient Tribes, the Conquest, the Colonial Period, Independence, the Texas War, and Porfirio Díaz and the Revolution--which give young readers a very good insight to Mexico's troubled history. It also indicts Mexico and the United States for the Texas War: "The events that led to the Texas War are numerous and complex, and it may be said, in all sincerity, that Mexico and the United States are equally to blame for the war, and for fostering the machinations and ambitions that finally caused the outbreak of hostilities" (p. 72).

*McClintock, Marshall. Prescott's The Conquest of Mexico. (New York: Julian Messner, 1948, 349 p.) Grades: 10-adult.

This is an abridgment of W. H. Prescott's The Conquest of Mexico. The editor has "designed for modern reading" Prescott's well-known, fast-moving drama of the conquest of Montezuma's vast Aztec Empire in central Mexico by Hernando Cortês and a handful of Europeans. It is interesting to note the point of view that Prescott chose to present in this book: Cortês is always described as an "extraordinary man." Alvarado and other Spanish conquerors are described as "underneath this showy exterior the future conqueror of Guatemala concealed a heart rash, rapacious, and cruel" (p. 201). And everything Aztec or from other native Mexican cultures is described as savage or barbaric. There are several pages devoted to the human sacrifices that were practiced by the Aztecs. After a thorough description of the sacrifice of the unhappy victims, the author states: "The most loathsome part

of the story is the manner in which the body of the
sacrificed captive was disposed of.   It was delivered
to the warrior who had taken him in battle and ... was
served up in an entertainment to his friends.   This
was not the coarse repast of famished cannibals....
Surely, never were refinement and the extreme of barbarism brought so closely in contact with each other!"
(p. 47).   The excitement and drama of the conquest of Mexico is indeed preserved in this book that reports the facts
from Cortês' perspective.   A lengthy account that may
interest serious readers.

Macgill, Hugh.   A Mexican Village: Life in a Zapotec
Community.   Edited by Paul J. Deegan.   Photos: Bruce
Larson.   (Mankato, Minnesota: Creative Educational
Society, 1970, 79 p.)   Grades: 4-8.

       Through excellent black-and-white photographs
and a well-researched text, this book describes the
town of Yalalag, which was founded by Zapotec Indians
in the high mountains of southern Mexico over four hundred years ago.   Yalalag, which did not have a road
until 1963, was accessible only by foot or by burro.
This isolation helped Yalalag maintain "its customs, its
costumes, its language and its Indian identity" (p. 5).
Despite "its myth and its romantic image" (p. 6), the
author does a very good job of portraying the harshness
of life in a Mexican town that lacks jobs and educational
opportunities, as well as newspapers and television.
The photographs depict cooking done on stones, burros
at work, restaurants that generally serve "only eggs,
beans, and tortillas" (p. 62), and shoeless Yalaltecos.

Madison, Winifred.   Maria Luisa.   (New York: J. B.
Lippincott Company, 1971, 187 p.)   Grades: 6-9.

       A story about a poor, unsophisticated Mexican-
American girl who goes to live with her aunt, uncle,
cousins, and grandmother in San Francisco.   It describes a very difficult situation for Maria Luisa and
her younger brother and their many problems.   Her

cousin explained to her: "It's a Mexican restaurant,
but nobody ever said it was for Chicanos. They
couldn't afford a glass of water there, that is, if they
could get by the front door" (p. 20). Or at school:
"'What are you anyway, a Mexican, a Cuban, or
what?'" "'You sure look Mexican. You sound it,
too,' Carol said" (p. 51). Her father was an alcoholic,
and her mother "had had a childhood of unbelievable
poverty, ten people living in two miserable rooms and
a father who could not find work" (p. 182).

*Neurath, Marie. They Lived Like This: The Ancient
Maya. Illus.: John Ellis. (New York: Franklin
Watts, 1966, 32 p.) Grades: 4-6.

        Authentic drawings based on Mayan wall paintings
and designs and a simple text describe outstanding aspects of Mayan civilization: pottery, agriculture, gods,
cities, religious buildings, pyramids, jewelry, ceremonies, wars, houses, astronomy, calendar, and
mathematics.

Nevins, Albert J. Away to Mexico. (New York:
Dodd, Mead & Company, 1966, 95 p.) Grades: 7-9.

        This book was copyrighted in 1966 by the Catho-
lic Foreign Mission Society of America, Inc. I pre-
sume that its purpose was to present one view of the
history of Mexico and its people. Many of the statistics
need to be updated. And, many of the assertions in
this book are insulting to Mexican people: "The goal
of every Mexican male is to be 'macho'--very much a
man. It is for this reason that so many Mexican men
wear a moustache. Machismo is a way of life and explains many things in the Mexican character" (p. 17).
This book emphasizes one aspect of Aztec culture:
"Religion was the center of Aztec life.... It was a
loathsome religion that demanded human sacrifice and
practiced cannibalism. It was this religion that filled
the Spanish with disgust for the Aztecs, which convinced them that the devil was at work and which was

to cause abuses on their part.   But the sight of an Aztec priest, his hair tangled and matted with dried blood,
plunging an obsidian knife into the chest of a captured
victim, tearing forth a still-pulsating heart and then
eating it, would fill any stranger with horror" (pp. 23-
24).   It tells about Mexico's important saints, the position of the Catholic Church, and other aspects of Mexican culture.   "Some of the foods that originated in
Mexico are tomatoes, squash, chili, vanilla beans,
maize, eggplant, pumpkin, peanuts, cashews, and avo-
cado" (p. 80).

*Newlon, Clarke.   The Men Who Made Mexico.   (New
York: Dodd, Mead & Company, 1973, 259 p.)   Grades:
7-12.

      Through Mexico's heroes this book introduces the
reader to Mexico's past and present.   It includes brief
and simple biographical sketches of the following Mexican heroes, artists, writers, politicians, and presidents: Miguel Hidalgo, La Corregidora, José María
Morelos, Agustín de Iturbide, Guadalupe Victoria, Antonio López de Santa Anna, Benito Juárez, Porfirio
Díaz, Francisco I. Madero, Pancho Villa, Emiliano
Zapata, Alvaro Obregón, Lázaro Cárdenas, José Vas-
concelos, Diego Rivera, Carlos Chávez, Cantinflas,
Martín Luis Guzmán, Pedro Ramírez Vásquez, Jorge
Pasquel, Antonio Ortiz Mena, Amalia Ledón, and Luis
Echeverría.
      The simple writing style and personal information
provided about each individual described in this book
make it a good background to the study of Mexico.   The
following is an example of how the author describes a
much-disliked Mexican: "Much has been written about
Santa Anna and his war with Texas, and much of it by
Texans or Texas sympathizers who tend to get hysteri-
cal at the mention of his name.... His transparent
willingness to trade off Texas in return for his own
safety, however, can be admired by no one" (pp. 97-
99).
      The weakest part of the book is the first chapter,
which tells about Mexican pre-Columbian cultures.   The

author needlessly emphasizes the Aztecs' practice of
human sacrifice and even condemns the Mayas in this
regard.

*Nolen, Barbara, editor.   Mexico Is People.   (New
York: Charles Scribner's Sons, 1973, 199 p.)   Grades:
9-adult.

Through brief writings of outstanding Mexican,
American, and European historians, scholars, and artists, the editor has put together a most enjoyable and
readable account of Mexico's pre-Columbian, colonial,
and revolutionary history, and its Fiestas, people, folk
and fine arts, and legends.   The brevity of the essays
and the interesting subjects described make this book a
genuine introduction to Mexico without many of the common misunderstandings.   For example, "The Bullfight"
is truly described as: 'It is all-important to remember
that there is no manner in bullfighting which has as its
object the infliction of pain upon the bull.   There is no
'teasing' of the animal ... the matador must kill it
bravely and with skill, and in order to kill it correctly
he must prepare the animal for death in an artistic,
yet dominating manner, risking his own life" (p. 51).
The editor selected authors who know many aspects of Mexico and its people, such as Miguel León-
Portilla, Bernal Díaz del Castillo, Octavio Paz, Martín
Luiz Guzmán, Américo Paredes, Frances Toor, and
others.

*O'Dell, Scott.   The King's Fifth.   (Boston: Houghton
Mifflin Company, 1966, 264 p.)   Grades: 9-12.

A well-written novel that includes excitement and
adventure in describing the Spaniards' search of Cíbola,
"cities where the houses were fashioned of gold and the
streets themselves paved with it, street after street"
(p. 14).   Most of the Spaniards are described as capable
of murder and any evil action in their frantic efforts to
obtain gold.   The author took some artistic liberties in
his reporting of the Spanish conquests.   Regarding Cortés

and the conquest of Mexico, he states: "He was the man who killed all the Aztecs. When he had killed them he made a law that no Indian can own a horse. Or ride upon a horse" (p. 48).

The conquerors' disappointments, quarrels, and vengeances are compared with the patience and understanding of the heroine Zia, an Indian girl, and a Spanish priest who could not understand the "sickness" in the minds of the conquerors.

Ogan, Margaret and George. Tennis Bum. (Philadelphia: The Westminster Press, 1976, 122 p.) Grades: 7-9.

A ridiculous story about a Chicano tennis player that includes too much tennis talk for readers who don't play tennis and too many artistic liberties for readers who play tennis well: Chico Gomez, the superficial tennis hero, is supposed to play championship tennis with both his left and right hands. This is an exaggeration that skillful tennis players will be quick to laugh at. The authors are also wrong about Mexican and South American liberators. Simón Bolívar was from Venezuela in South America. He never fought in Mexico as the authors mistakenly state: "In one of the revolutions down there, someone had shot off his left ear" (p. 7).

Even though the authors included "a seventeen-year-old Chicano on the run" with an alcoholic mother, gamblers that fix tennis matches, a suspicious black young tennis player, and a delightful and most understanding white tennis coach, this story will bore good tennis players and insult intelligent readers.

*Piggott, Juliet. Mexican Folk Tales. (New York: Crane Russak, 1973, 128 p.) Grades: 4-adult.

Excellent collection of eleven tales, mostly from pre-Columbian Mexico. The introduction gives a very good account of the swift success of the conquest of Mexico by the Spaniards. It is important to note that several of the tales emphasize the wisdom that pre-

Columbian people admired in their leaders: "Jiculi, Prince of the Huichol tribe ... was a young man, endowed with wisdom, modesty, and practicality beyond his years" (p. 32). And the story told of Tepoztecatl when he cut his way out of Xochicalcatl's stomach, "But all Tepoztecatl had to say about it at the time was: 'I am nearly a man'" (p. 128).

The attractive pre-Columbian illustrations and authentic tales offer a true introduction to the fascinating culture of Mexico. The book retells such well known tales as "Popocatepetl and Ixtlaccihuatl"; popular animal tales, like "The Rabbit and the Two Coyotes"; and some that explain the mystery of the world's creation, such as "A Story of a Flood" and "The Golden Man and the Finger Man, " which explains why "there would be rich men and poor men on the earth ... and that they would all fill the heavens with their praises... " (p. 56).

Pine, Tillie S. , and Joseph Levine.　The Mayans Knew. Illus.: Ann Grifalconi. (New York: McGraw-Hill Book Company, 1971, 38 p.) Grades: 3-6.

This book is divided into three parts: It briefly describes what the Maya knew and did; it explains that knowledge in today's terms; and it tells young readers what they may do to use that knowledge. The most interesting part tells about many things that the Maya knew and did. It tells how they built beautiful stone temples and large cities; developed a writing system; made paper and wrote books; invented a remarkable number system; studied astronomy and made an accurate calendar; used rubber for shoes and made rubber balls; and made several kinds of musical instruments.

*Pope, Billy N. , and Ramona Ware Emmons.　Your World: Let's Visit Mexico City. (Texas: Taylor Publishing Company, 1968, 30 p.) Grades: K-2.

Two girls from Texas and their mother take a train ride to Mexico City. They are invited into the

home of a very nice Mexican family.   The Mexican
girls' beautiful clothes, furniture, and home are a welcome contrast to many books that show only the poverty
in Mexico.   Together, they visit Mexico City's interesting sites: the Cathedral, Plaza of the Three Cultures,
Palace of Fine Arts, attractive statues, streets, parks,
the Aztec Stadium, the zoo, the floating gardens, the
pyramids, small shops, open markets, and the breaking
of a "pinata" [sic].   Attractive, large pictures in color
show the beauty of Mexico City.   The book ends by
stating: "We will remember our trip to Mexico City
for a long time.   It is the oldest city in North America.
Would you like to visit Mexico City?"   Perhaps young
children will indeed be enticed.

*Prago, Albert.   Strangers in Their Own Land: A His-
tory of Mexican-Americans.   (New York: Four Winds
Press, 1973, 206 p.)   Grades: 9-12.

By combining the history of Mexico and the history of the southwest United States, the author hopes to
explain the reasons why the "Mexican-American is considered inferior and his customs mocked or, at best,
tolerated in a patronizing way" (pp. 6-7).   This book
recounts the conquest of Mexico and the Southwest by the
Spaniards; Mexico's independence, and the conquest of
the Southwest by the Americans.   It briefly narrates the
lives of Juárez, Zapata, Villa, César Chávez, and Rodol-
fo Gonzáles.   In a simple, easy-to-understand manner
the author emphasizes the differences and problems that
the Spaniards encountered in colonizing the Southwest and
the conditions of life in the Southwest during the nineteenth century.   For example, in 1836 "there were no
schools in California except the mission-operated schools
for religious indoctrination.   There were no newspapers,
libraries, theatres, museums or any other such cultural
resources" (p. 77).
The author is impatient with the life of the
"campesinos" of the Southwest: "The migrant workers
remain the worst housed, the worst paid, and the most
exploited labor force in the nation" (p. 189), and reports
that "a growing militancy among Mexican-Americans ...

along with those of other minorities ... contain the ex-
plosive elements of what may be a new American Revolution" (p. 206).

*Rink, Paul. Warrior Priests and Tyrant Kings: The
Beginnings of Mexican Independence.   (New York:
Doubleday and Company, 1976, 180 p.) Grades: 8-10.

     This book is a good overview of the causes, af-
termath, and major personalities of Mexico's fight for
independence in the nineteenth century.   Especially well
described are the efforts of Mexico's leaders, such as
Hidalgo, Morelos, and Iturbide.   Unfortunately, it contains too much information for young readers unfamiliar
with Mexico's history: it examines in some depth
Spain's role as a great power in the sixteenth century
as well as the abuses of the Catholic Church in the
New World.   The author is very forthright in his description of some of Mexico's controversial patriots.
The following is a sample of what the author thinks of
Agustín de Iturbide: "the dashing and handsome de Iturbide became the first of a long line of opportunistic,
self-seeking 'leaders' who did so much to tear down the
good work accomplished by Mexico's true and selfless
patriots.   The greed and vanity of men such as he are
in stark contrast to the simple honor and dignity of people like los padres Hidalgo and Morelos.   The damage
they did has been a heavy load, in fact at times seem-
ing almost too heavy, for the people of the struggling
nation to carry" (p. 151).   (Many Mexican historians
agree with this author.)
     The name Agostín [sic] de Iturbide is misspelled
throughout the book.

Rosenblum, Morris.   Heroes of Mexico.   (New York:
Fleet Press Corporation, 1969, 139 p.) Grades: 7-12.

     This book contains seventeen brief biographies
of outstanding men and women from Mexico.   The author included three pre-Columbian heroes: Quetzalcoatl,
Montezuma, and Cuauhtémoc; the following heroes and

heroines of Mexico's colonial, independence and revolutionary times: Sor Juana Inês de la Cruz, Miguel Hidalgo, Francisco Javier Mina, Vicente Guerrero, Benito
Juárez, Pancho Villa, Emiliano Zapata, and Lázaro
Cárdenas; the artists José Clemente Orozco and Diego
Rivera; and the musician Carlos Chávez. Unfortunately,
many of the photographs are too dark and obscure.
However, the author's simple style and objectivity in
portraying the lives of the people make this book a good
introduction to some of Mexico's heroes. The following
is a sample of the author's veracity in describing controversial people: "There are different opinions about
Pancho Villa. To some persons he was a murderer
and a bandit. To others he was a fool who had impossible dreams. To still others he was a great guerilla
fighter who fought for the good of the poor people" (p.
98).

*Sandoval, Ruben. Games Games Games. Photos:
David Strick. (New York: Doubleday and Company,
1977, 78 p.) Grades: K-6.

     As expressed by the authors, the "purpose of
this book is to help maintain the continuity between the
games of Mexico and the newer ones played in the bar-
rios of California, and thus to help preserve a truly bilingual and bicultural tradition in the United States" (p.
13). The outstanding black-and-white photographs of
happy Mexican-American children at play in the barrio
can be enjoyed by anyone. A few of the delightful
rhymes, amusing tongue twisters, and diverting games
that Mexican children have known for several generations are indeed preserved in this handsome book.

Shannon, Terry. ...and Juan. Illus.: Charles Payzant. (Chicago: Albert Whitman and Company, 1961,
48 p.) Grades: 3-5.

     An absurd book that was written with a good in-
tention: to show how folk arts and crafts are being
carried on in many Mexican villages by whole families.

However, the illustrations and text include many ridiculous Mexican stereotypes. Siestas: "Everyone slept in
the peaceful warmth of the early afternoon. . . . Even
the goats and the burros dozed on the hillsides" (p. 5).
Obviously, it has the most appropriate illustration of
sombreroed, sandaled, and sleeping peasants. Poverty:
"When business was bad, Juan and the others contented
themselves with smaller servings of beans and fewer
tortillas" (p. 9). Does anyone really believe this statement? The text mentions "the City, " where the children and Papa "arranged their pottery on straw mats
under a canopy in the open air" (p. 31). The author
is here being absurd one more time: she meant a
Mexican village. And, the final insult to Mexico's arti-
sans: Juan is saved by a turista. He "brushed the
tears from his eyes the better to watch the woman count
the centavos into Papa's hand. At last someone wanted
the splendid horse he had made" (p. 47).

*Shellabarger, Samuel. Captain from Castile. (Boston:
Little, Brown and Company, 1945, 503 p.) Grades:
7-12.

By taking many artistic liberties the author has
recreated the fascinating adventure, terror, and excitement of life in Spain in the sixteenth century, as well
as the passion and turbulence of the conquest of Mexico.
Through the life of a dashing young Spaniard, Pedro de
Vargas, the reader experiences the fanatical horror of
the Inquisition in Spain; the beauty and animation of life
with Montezuma, Cortés, and Doña Marina in Tenochti-
tlán (Mexico City); love; and the triumph of a valiant
conquistador in the palace of Charles of Austria. An
absorbing novel that will enthrall young readers in spite
of its length.

*Singer, Jane and Kurt. Folk Tales of Mexico. (Minne-
apolis: T. S. Denison & Company, 1969, 110 p.)
Grades: 4-10.

Outstanding collection of ten Mexican folk tales,
drawn from pre-Columbian times through the Mexican

Revolution, that highlight important beliefs of Mexican
people.   It includes well-known pre-Columbian legends:
Quetzalcóatl--the Plumed Serpent; Ixtlacihuatl and Popo-
catépetl; Yallo, the Wise Fool (a Zapotec legend); and
How the Earth Was Created (A Mayan legend).   From
the colonial period it includes the legend of the China
Poblana and the Legend of the Virgin of Guadalupe.
From the nineteenth century it includes a legend of
Benito Juárez.   From the twentieth century: "How
Pancho Villa Sold His Soul to El Diablo."
        This is a marvelous introduction to Mexico and
its history through Mexico's fascinating folk tales.

Smith, Garry and Vesta.   Poco.   Illus.:   Fred Crump,
Jr.   (N.p.:   Prism Press, 1975, 28 p.)   Grades: K-2.

        Black-and-white illustrations show the typical
"burros loaded with wares," peasants with large som-
breros and a great variety of attractive birds, as we
follow Poco, a tiny cactus wren, and his adventures as
he flies to the market in Mexico City to find his uncle
who has been caged by a bird seller.   When he reached
the market, Poco saw "warm tortillas, spicy chiles,
juicy frijoles" and other curios, and, as is to be expected: "The fortune teller is taking a nap in the
shade...."   (Spanish translation: "El adivino está to-
mando una siesta....")   An attractive animal story without the "Mexican curios."   The story is completely
translated into readable Spanish with a few misspellings:
"Carquados" [sic], "Supon que" [sic].

Summers, James L.   You Can't Make It by Bus.   (Philadelphia: The Westminster Press, 1969, 174 p.)
Grades: 7-12.

        The author tried very hard to write a love story
about Paul Guevara, a Mexican-American teenage boy
who is in constant search for his "true identity" and
Lura Golden, a Jewish girl who is intelligent and pretty,
but obviously submissive.   The story also includes violent Chicanos from East Los Angeles; liberal teachers
who believed "in due process, the Fourteenth Amendment,

and the Bill of Rights" (p. 49); and uninspiring Mexican Americans who believe in hard work but can't seem to convince anyone.

A trip to Guadalajara emphasizes the poverty and negative aspects of Mexico: "Paul Guevara was stunned, his eyes fixed on the miserable hovels along the road, where naked children and dogs inhabited the littered yards" (p. 120).   There are also descriptions of "Mordida ... 'It's how you do it down here'" (p. 123); and Mexican men who insult beautiful girls: "They were men, and this was Mexico" (p. 128).   Paul Guevara is supposed to "discover himself" after such a trip; nonetheless, violence triumphs.

*Werstein, Irving.   Land and Liberty.   (New York: Cowles Book Company, 1971, 207 p.)   Grades: 10-adult.

The author sought to illuminate for young readers the story of the Mexican Revolution, 1910-1919.   All the main characters that participated in Mexico's violent revolution are described with strong words, such as Mexico's president-turned-dictator Porfirio Díaz: "Indeed, he ruled over Mexico like a medieval despot. Those rash or foolish enough to have opposed him in the past frequently had wound up in front of a firing squad" (p. 3).   General Victoriano Huerta "had an insatiable yen for cognac and drank incredible quantities of it every day" (p. 79).   Venustiano Carranza "was domineering, egotistical, and remarkably ignorant of the history and needs of the people whom he proposed to govern" (p. 113).   President Woodrow Wilson's interference in Mexico's political situation is described, as well as Wilson's personal agent John Lind, who "believed that the main causes of Mexico's troubles were the Catholic Church, tequila, and prostitution, in that order" (p. 129).   The author uses many unbelievable quotes without citing any sources for them!   They do make for amusing reading, but I wonder about them. The following is a quote attributed to Pancho Villa, who was pleading with American authorities to let him have Castillo, a Mexican bandit: "I'll give him a fair hear-

ing, ' Villa promised. 'He can have a lawyer, a judge,
and a jury. Then I'll shoot him' " (p. 137). This book
is indeed a readable account of the Mexican Revolution,
but one must at times question its authenticity.

Whitney, Phyllis A. A Long Time Coming. (New York:
David McKay Company, 1954, 261 p.) Grades: 7-12.

This book reflects a naive outlook on life that
fortunately is not appreciated by teenagers today.
Christie, the eighteen-year-old daughter of an absentee
plant owner, resolves to help the migrant workers employed by her father's plant. She is supported by a
handsome prince, Tom Webb, who is also an outspoken
reporter and who eventually asks her for a date. It
includes other "good" characters, such as a young min-
ister and a social worker, and a "bad" aunt, Miss
Amelia Allard, who dislikes Mexicans because of " 'the
dirt, the smells, the ignorance, the disease.... You
can't tell me trouble isn't brewing when you find eight
or ten teen-age Mexican boys hanging around on street
corners with nothing to do' " (pp. 58-59).
The town and the Mexican and Mexican-American
migrant workers have serious problems, but the author
finds an unbelievably simple solution and: " 'Everything's
going to be all right!' Christie cried, waving both hands
at Aurora, who saw her and waved back" (p. 260).

Witton, Dorothy. Teen-age Mexican Stories. (New
York: Lantern Press Inc., Publishers, 1972, 167 p.)
Grades: 7-10.

This is a collection of six stories that take place
in various parts of Mexico. Unfortunately, the author
is obviously only acquainted with well-known tourist attractions and describes Mexican people from the view-
point of a tourist; the stories are not, as she states in
the introduction, "about the conflicts of some ... Mexican young people who are caught between the narrow
traditional way of life and the broad new world that is
opening up to them" (p. 6). Witton does not understand

Mexican traditions, nor the conflicts of Mexican people.
Her stories tell about pottery making, friendship, life
in a Mexican village, selling clay idols to the tourists,
and lives of extreme poverty with the constant emphasis
on beans and tortillas and the "kindness of American
tourists. " Perhaps a tourist guidebook might give a
better introduction to Mexican tourist attractions than
this collection of depressing stories.

Young, Bob and Jan. Across the Tracks. (New York:
Julian Messner, 1958, 192 p.) Grades: 7-9.

        Betty Ochoa, a Mexican-American girl who lives
in Los Angeles, is successful in many areas of her life:
she has a happy family life; she is a good student in
school; she is elected activities commissioner at school;
and she wins a scholarship to go to college.   It is refreshing to be exposed to a middle-class Mexican-American family that demonstrates many positive values, even
though the authors felt compelled to explain that Betty's
mother: "unlike many Latin women ... had not added
weight with the years" (p. 19) and make similar un-
called for explanations regarding "nice" Mexican-American people.
        Betty's feelings about her own Mexican background
and Mexican friends, as well as her normal fears and
doubts, make this a "nice" story about an average teen-
age girl.   The following words in Spanish are misspelled: "emplanadas" (p. 59) and "Los Posadas" (p.
131).

BOOKS REVIEWED IN THIS CHAPTER:

Atwater, James D. , and Ramón Eduardo Ruiz.   Out
    From Under: Benito Juárez and the Struggle for
    Mexican Independence.   Illus.:   Paul Hogarth.   (New
    York: Doubleday and Company, 1969, 111 p.)
    Grades: 6-12.

Baker, Betty.   No Help At All.   Illus.:   Emily Arnold

McCully. (New York: Greenwillow Books, 1978,
56 p.) Grades: K-2.

Baker, Betty. Walk the World's Rim. (New York:
Harper & Row, 1965, 168 p.) Grades: 5-8.

*Baker, Nina Brown. Juárez, Hero of Mexico. Illus.:
Marion Greenwood. (New York: The Vanguard
Press, 1942, 308 p.) Grades: 7-12.

Bannon, Laura. Manuela's Birthday. (Chicago: Albert
Whitman, 1972, 30 p.) Grades: K-3.

*Beck, Barbara L. The First Book of the Aztecs. Il-
lus.: Page Cary. (New York: Franklin Watts,
1977, 67 p.) Grades: 4-6.

Caldwell, John C. Let's Visit Mexico. (New York:
The John Day Company, 1965, 95 p.) Grades: 3-7.

Carr, Harriett H. The Mystery of the Aztec Idol.
(New York: The Macmillan Company, 1959, 193 p.)
Grades: 4-6.

Cox, William. Chicano Cruz. (New York: Bantam
Books, 1972, 216 p.) Grades: 6-12.

Dedera, Don, and Bob Robles. Goodbye García Adiós.
(Flagstaff, Ariz.: Northland Press, 1976, 117 p.)
Grades: 7-12.

Dunnahoo, Terry. This is Espie Sanchez. (New York:
E. P. Dutton & Co., 1976, 156 p.) Grades: 4-7.

Dunnahoo, Terry. Who Needs Espie Sanchez? (New
York: E. P. Dutton & Co., 1977, 138 p.) Grades:
6-9.

Epstein, Sam and Beryl. The First Book of Mexico.
(New York: Franklin Watts, 1976, 86 p.) Grades:
4-6.

Friskey, Margaret. Welcome to Mexico. Illus.: Lois

Axeman. (Chicago: Children's Press, 1975, 48 p.)
Grades: 2-5.

Grace, Nancy. Earrings for Celia. Illus.: Helen
Siegl (New York: Pantheon, 1963, 46 p.) Grades:
3-5.

Hancock, Ralph. Mexico. (New York: The Macmillan
Company, 1964, 117 p.) Grades: 6-9.

Herman, Vic. Juanito's Railroad in the Sky. Illus.:
Vic Herman. (New York: Golden Press, 1976, 61
p.) Grades: 2-6.

*Hobart, Lois. Mexican Mural: The Story of Mexico,
Past and Present. (New York: Harcourt, Brace &
World, 1963, 211 p.) Grades: 9-12.

Jennings, Gary. The Rope in the Jungle. (New York:
J. B. Lippincott Company, 1976, 225 p.) Grades:
5-7.

Kalnay, Francis. It Happened in Chichipica. Illus.:
Charles Robinson. (New York: Harcourt Brace
Jovanovich, 1971, 127 p.) Grades: 4-6.

Kirtland, G. B. One Day in Aztec Mexico. Illus.:
Jerome Snyder. (New York: Harcourt, Brace &
World, 1963, 38 p.) Grades: 4-6.

*Kouzel, Daisy. The Cuckoo's Reward. El Premio del
Cuco. Illus.: Earl Thollander. (New York: Doubleday and Company, 1977, 28 p.) Grades: K-3.

*Larralde, Elsa. The Land and People of Mexico. (New
York: J. B. Lippincott Company, 1964, 158 p.)
Grades: 6-12.

*McClintock, Marshall. Prescott's The Conquest of Mex-
ico. (New York: Julian Messner, 1948, 349 p.)
Grades: 10-adult.

Macgill, Hugh. A Mexican Village: Life in a Zapotec

Community. Edited by Paul J. Deegan. Photos:
Bruce Larson. (Mankato, Minnesota: Creative Educational Society, 1970, 79 p.) Grades: 4-8.

Madison, Winifred. Maria Luisa. (New York: J. B.
Lippincott Company, 1971, 187 p.) Grades: 6-9.

*Neurath, Marie. They Lived Like This: The Ancient
Maya. Illus.: John Ellis. (New York: Franklin
Watts, 1966, 32 p.) Grades: 4-6.

Nevins, Albert J. Away to Mexico. (New York:
Dodd, Mead & Company, 1966, 95 p.) Grades: 7-9.

*Newlon, Clarke. The Men Who Made Mexico. (New
York: Dodd, Mead & Company, 1973, 259 p.)
Grades: 7-12.

*Nolen, Barbara, editor. Mexico Is People. (New
York: Charles Scribner's Sons, 1973, 199 p.)
Grades: 9-adult.

*O'Dell, Scott. The King's Fifth. (Boston: Houghton
Mifflin Company, 1966, 264 p.) Grades: 9-12.

Ogan, Margaret and George. Tennis Bum. (Philadelphia: The Westminster Press, 1976, 122 p.)
Grades: 7-9.

*Piggott, Juliet. Mexican Folk Tales. (New York:
Crane Russak, 1973, 128 p.) Grades: 4-adult.

Pine, Tillie S., and Joseph Levine. The Mayans Knew.
Illus.: Ann Grifalconi. (New York: McGraw-Hill
Book Company, 1971, 38 p.) Grades: 3-6.

*Pope, Billy N., and Ramona Ware Emmons. Your
World: Let's Visit Mexico City. (Texas: Taylor
Publishing Company, 1968, 30 p.) Grades: K-2.

*Prago, Albert. Strangers in Their Own Land: A His-
tory of Mexican-Americans. (New York: Four
Winds Press, 1973, 206 p.) Grades: 9-12.

*Rink, Paul. Warrior Priests and Tyrant Kings: The Beginnings of Mexican Independence. (New York: Doubleday and Company, 1976, 180 p.) Grades: 8-10.

Rosenblum, Morris. Heroes of Mexico. (New York: Fleet Press Corporation, 1969, 139 p.) Grades: 7-12.

*Sandoval, Ruben. Games Games Games. Photos: David Strick. (New York: Doubleday and Company, 1977, 78 p.) Grades: K-6.

Shannon, Terry. ...and Juan. Illus.: Charles Payzant. (Chicago: Albert Whitman and Company, 1961, 48 p.) Grades: 3-5.

*Shellabarger, Samuel. Captain from Castile. (Boston: Little, Brown and Company, 1945, 503 p.) Grades: 7-12.

*Singer, Jane and Kurt. Folk Tales of Mexico. (Minneapolis: T. S. Denison & Company, 1969, 110 p.) Grades: 4-10.

Smith, Garry and Vesta. Poco. Illus.: Fred Crump, Jr. (N.p.: Prism Press, 1975, 28 p.) Grades: K-2.

Summers, James L. You Can't Make It by Bus. (Philadelphia: The Westminster Press, 1969, 174 p.) Grades: 7-12.

*Werstein, Irving. Land and Liberty. (New York: Cowles Book Company, 1971, 207 p.) Grades: 10-adult.

Whitney, Phyllis A. A Long Time Coming. (New York: David McKay Company, 1954, 261 p.) Grades: 7-12.

Witton, Dorothy. Teen-Age Mexican Stories. (New York: Lantern Press, 1972, 167 p.) Grades: 7-10.

Young, Bob and Jan. Across the Tracks. (New York: Julian Messner, 1958, 192 p.) Grades: 7-9.

PANAMA (AND CENTRAL AMERICA)

Panama is a narrow isthmus connecting North (or Central) and South America. The principal reason for Panama's existence as a nation, and the principal source of its earnings, is the Panama Canal. More than half of the population, the nation's capital (Panama), and other major cities are found near the Canal. In 1903 a French company, with the knowledge of the United States, engineered a revolution that guaranteed Panama's independence from Colombia. The United States recognized the independence of Panama three days after its proclamation on November 3, 1903. Shortly thereafter the United States started construction of the interoceanic canal across the isthmus.

Panama has a population of under two million. Most of its people are mulatto (mixed African and European background), although Spanish customs and architecture are very prominent. African, native Indian, and Spanish influences have resulted in colorful folk dances, accented by West Indian songs and rhythms.

Bananas are Panama's main crop and chief commercial product, followed by rice, corn, coffee, and sugarcane.

There are many controversial issues in Panama and the United States concerning the status of the Panama Canal: In Panama some groups oppose the presence of the United States in the Canal Zone and would like the United States to withdraw completely. Other groups would prefer that the United States continue ad-

ministering and operating the Canal with increased yearly payments.   In the United States some groups argue
that the North Americans have inherent rights in Panama, since there would be no canal without U.S. help,
while other groups maintain that the Canal is now obsolete for modern trade and military use and therefore
favor giving control of the Canal to Panama.

The following books will introduce students to
Panama, Central America, and the Panama Canal.
(Asterisks indicate noteworthy books.)

Caldwell, John C.   Let's Visit Central America.   (New
York: The John Day Company, 1964 ["Data in this edition brought up to date, 1973"(?)], 94 p.)   Grades:
3-7.

The author's opinions about Central America's
problems are interspersed with descriptions of the history and life in the various countries, with just a few
added paragraphs to update superficially the 1964 data.
There is an interesting chapter on the story of the Panama Canal: "The French spent money on a firm of
New York lawyers, and they sent long telegrams to
members of Congress.   Most engineers believed that
route across Nicaragua was best because there were
two big lakes that could be used as a part of the route.
Yet the French were able to change the minds of many
Congressmen" (p. 10), continuing with a report on how
the Canal functions.   In the chapter on plantations in
Central America the author states about the United Fruit
Company: "All through its plantations, it has built
company villages and towns so that its workers may
have good housing. . . .   When I visited United Fruit
Company plantations in Central America I noticed that
the company workers had much better houses than other
people living nearby . . . we should also think of big
companies like the United Fruit Company as providing
foreign aid" (pp. 73-74).   I am sure that many Central
American economists disagree with many of Caldwell's
suggestions.

Carpenter, Allan. Enchantment of Panama. (Chicago:
Children's Press, 1971, 88 p.)   Grades: 5-9.

   An interesting and well-written book about Panama that describes its geography, history, natural resources, people, and tourist attractions.   It narrates
simply the importance of the Canal to Panama and the
world.   Unfortunately, it only discusses the problems
associated with the Canal until 1970.   Excellent background material that should be supplemented with recent
readings about Panama and the Canal.

Clayton, Robert. Mexico, Central America and the
West Indies. (New York: The John Day Company,
1970, 45 p.)   Grades: 4-8.

   This is a brief introduction to Mexico, Central
America, and the West Indies emphasizing their vegetation, winds, and agricultural production.   The simple
charts and maps that describe the temperature, winds,
and raw materials of several of these countries are the
best part of the book.   The author stresses the role of
the United States, for example: "... Puerto Rico was
ceded by Spain to the United States in 1898, and much
of the island's present prosperity is due to the close
ties with the United States....   The government has
also helped industrial expansion, again with aid from
the U.S.A. " (p. 24).   And so on....

Day, Dee. Getting to Know Panama. Illus. :   Don
Lambo. (New York: Coward-McCann, 1958, 61 p.)
Grades: 2-4.

   In very simple language the author gives a brief
introduction to Panama and its people.   It tells why the
U. S. Senators and Representatives chose to build the
canal in Panama; it describes the canal's huge concrete
passageways, called "locks"; it tells about the Cunas
and San Blas Indians' customs; and it describes several
fiestas in Panama.   This book may be useful as a historical overview to Panama and the Canal if students
are exposed to additional current information.

Karen, Ruth. The Land and People of Central America.
(New York: J. B. Lippincott Company, 1965 [revised
1972], 157 p.) Grades: 6-10.

In strong, emotional language the author describes the history and problems of Guatemala, El Salvador, Honduras, Nicaragua, Costa Rica, and Panama.
For example: ". . . three centuries of Castilian rule left
them with the remains of a feudal social structure and
the Spanish tradition of violence in politics and corrup-
tion in high places" (p. 22). and: "Not until the beginning of the Good Neighbor Policy in the nineteen thirties
did the United States really look at, let alone like, its
little neighbors on the isthmus. Mainly it ignored
them. Sometimes it bullied them. When needed, it
was not available, and often it meddled where no one
wanted it" (p. 53). The author defends the much-
criticized banana companies: "They did not plunder;
they planted--efficiently, extensively, and expansively.
In a country [Honduras] where no one else was doing
much of anything, the banana companies soon became a
power simply by being energetic and being there" (p.
84). The author writes very highly of democratic Costa
Rica, and condemns Panama's Spanish conquerors for
encouraging "in the Spanish settlers an economic attitude
that has haunted Panama ever since. Padrias held that
Panama's geographic position made it a natural trade
route, and that all its people had to do was to sit back
and profit from the commerce which must needs come
their way" (pp. 119-20).
        This is the author's explanation for Panama's
"independence" from Colombia: "But the country did
not gain its freedom finally until 1903, when Colombian
blindness and cupidity over the matter of the Panama
Canal pushed Panamanian resentment to the point of no
return and brought the newly proclaimed republic imme-
diate recognition and long-range protection from the
United States" (p. 120).
        Surely many people in Central America will dis-
agree with many of the author's assertions about their
countries.

Monjo, F. N. <u>Pirates in Panama</u>. Illus.: Wallace Tripp. (New York: Simon and Schuster, 1970, 62 p.) Grades: 3-4.

This is an amusing version of the story of the pirate Henry Morgan and his visit to Panama in 1671. Brother John and Benito were very proud of their Altar of Gold. So, when the pirates came to take all the gold from the people in Panama, Brother John and Benito whitewashed their beloved altar, and according to legend, Morgan gave Brother John ten thousand pieces of gold for the altar. The author's emphasis on a heroic burro and angry bulls detracts from the original legend as told to children in Panama.

*Moser, Don. <u>Central American Jungles</u>. (New York: Time-Life Books, 1975, 179 p.) Grades: 7-12.

The enchanting wilderness of Central America is marvelously described for the reader through the author's interesting experiences and superb color photographs of excellent Time-Life quality. The luxuriant complexity and abundance of life of the Central American countries (Guatemala, El Salvador, Honduras, Nicaragua, Costa Rica, Panama, and Belize) are depicted in captivating detail. The book describes the land, volcanoes, mountains, vegetation, birds, monkeys, coast swamps, wild animals, and forests. The following is an example of how vividly the author tells about life in the jungle: "I was stunned by the speed and ease with which the ants had killed the scorpion. It had been no contest at all. I felt a little uneasy standing right in the midst of the columns, but Jim assured me that the ants were no danger to humans or other large animals--we could simply move out of range in a few steps.... The ants raid human habitations at the edge of the jungle periodically, he said, and when this happens the people clear out. Such raids are not regarded as unmitigated evils, for the ants clean out cockroaches and other vermin as thoroughly as any exterminator might" (p. 93).

Panama and the Canal Zone in Pictures. (New York:
Sterling Publishing Company, 1977, 64 p.) Grades:
7-12.

      This is a simple overview of Panama and the
Canal Zone with pictures from the 1950s and early
1960s.   The text very briefly describes the land, history, government, people, and economy.   The editors
seem to update every few years the section on "The
United States and the Canal" by adding a few paragraphs describing the recent developments.   Even though
it simplifies important issues in the United States and
Panama, it does provide the reader with a simple understanding of the treaties until September 7, 1977,
when "Presidents Carter and Torrijos signed two treaties
that would transfer control of the Canal and Canal Zone
to Panama by the year 2000" (p. 39).

Rink, Paul.   The Land Divided, The World United.
Illus.: Barry Martin.   (New York: Julian Messner,
1963, 179 p.)   Grades: 7-10.

      This is the story of the Panama Canal starting
with the Spanish settlements in the sixteenth century
until the increased yearly rental in 1955.   It includes
interesting episodes connected with the building of the
Canal, such as Ferdinand de Lesseps's unsuccessful attempt in 1887 and President Roosevelt's controversial
role in extending recognition to the new nation.   It discusses the importance of the Panama Canal to the United
States by comparing it to the Suez Canal: "Theoretical-
ly, the Suez Canal is an 'international' canal, and in
times of war is available to the ships of any nation--
warships or merchant vessels.   The Panama Canal is a
'private' canal.   It belongs to us.   In wartime it is
open only to our own ships and those of our allies.
We defend it and patrol its approaches to see that this
is so.   This seems reasonable and yet many thinking
people say this is wrong.   They say that control of a
great interocean waterway, which benefits all mankind,
should not be in the hands of any one nation" (pp. 176-
77).

BOOKS REVIEWED IN THIS CHAPTER:

Caldwell, John C. Let's Visit Central America. (New
York: The John Day Company, 1964, 94 p.)
Grades: 3-7.

Carpenter, Allan. Enchantment of Panama. (Chicago:
Children's Press, 1971, 88 p.) Grades: 5-9.

Clayton, Robert. Mexico, Central America and the
West Indies. (New York: The John Day Company,
1970, 45 p.) Grades: 4-8.

Day, Dee. Getting to Know Panama. Illus.: Don
Lambo. (New York: Coward-McCann, 1958, 61 p.)
Grades: 2-4.

Karen, Ruth. The Land and People of Central America.
(New York: J. B. Lippincott Company, 1965 [re-
vised 1972], 157 p.) Grades: 6-10.

Monjo, F. N. Pirates in Panama. Illus.: Wallace
Tripp. (New York: Simon and Schuster, 1970, 62
p.) Grades: 3-4.

*Moser, Don. Central American Jungles. (New York:
Time-Life Books, 1975, 179 p.) Grades: 7-12.

Panama and the Canal Zone in Pictures. (New York:
Sterling Publishing Company, 1977, 64 p.) Grades:
7-12.

Rink, Paul. The Land Divided, The World United.
Illus.: Barry Martin. (New York: Julian Messner,
1963, 179 p.) Grades: 7-10.

PERU

Peru is the third–largest country in South America and has 1,400 miles of Pacific Ocean coastline. The country is divided into three well-defined regions: the coastal area, which is arid or semi-arid, includes Lima, the capital, and much of the industrial, commercial, and agricultural activity; the Andes Mountains occupy about 27 percent of Peru's land area and are the principal barrier to transportation and communication between the coast and the interior; and the isolated eastern lowlands occupy more than half of Peru's total land area. Numerous rivers, which wind their way to the Amazon River, are the only transportation routes in the area.

There are three major ethnic groups in Peru: the Indians make up about 46 percent of the population; mestizo (European-Indian), 38 percent; and white, 16 percent. Even after four hundred years of contact, these groups still retain much of their distinctive characters and traditional divisions. The literacy rate is about 50 percent, despite a new education law that makes education free and compulsory for both sexes between the ages of seven and sixteen.

Peru formed the nucleus of the highly developed Inca civilization, which emerged in the eleventh or early twelfth century. Centered at Cuzco, the Inca Empire extended over a vast region from northern Ecuador to central Chile. The Incas were great artists. They produced beautiful textiles and ceramics. They also achieved a high degree of engineering knowledge, as evidenced by great cities (Machu Picchu and Cuzco), magnificent bridges and roads, huge stone buildings, and farming terraces.

The Spaniards, in search of Inca wealth, founded Lima in 1535. Lima became the most distinguished and aristocratic colonial capital, as well as the chief stronghold, in South America.

Even though Peru has been famous for its rich and varied mineral resources, nearly half the population works in agriculture. Most of the Indians are engaged in subsistence farming, largely in the mountains, where there is a lack of schools, food, housing, transportation, and communication. The fishing industry has become an important activity in recent decades, making fish and fish products major items of export.

The following books will introduce students to the marvelous Inca culture and to modern Peru. (Asterisks indicate noteworthy books.)

*Baumann, Hans. Gold and Gods of Peru. Translated by Stella Humphries. (New York: Pantheon, 1963, 201 p.) Grades: 9-12.

The fascinating world of the Incas and other pre-Columbian civilizations of Peru are described for the reader through original historical sources and beautiful color photographs and drawings. Of special interest is the chapter "Felipillo's Story, " which tells of Pizarro's conquest of Peru as narrated by Pizarro's interpreter, the Indian boy Felipillo. The author must be commended for reporting differing views about the Inca rulers as viewed by their contemporaries: "The Sons of the Sun built a house for their nation on which the sun could shine peacefully. Their kingdom was indeed great and the Incas were good rulers. I, Felipe Huaman Poma de Ayala, say so.... I, Pedro de Sarmiento de Gamboa, say that the Incas were bad rulers.... We Spaniards have often been represented as devils who brought all kinds of misery to the natives of Peru, but

I know that we freed them from slavery. I have con-
ducted hearings throughout the land and I am in a position to say just what despots these Incas really were.
They were tyrants who exploited their own people and
the many subject tribes as well" (pp. 86-87). On page
34 there is a mistake regarding a date connected with
Atahualpa's residence: September 1953 is surely
wrong!

Bleeker, Sonia. The Inca, Indians of the Andes. Illus. :   Patricia Boodell. (New York: William Morrow
and Company, 1960, 150 p.) Grades: 4-6.

In a simple, easy-to-understand manner the author narrates Inca conquests, the Inca highway, the Inca
at home, growing up, farming, the crafts of the empire,
beliefs and ceremonies, and the last of the Inca.   Un-
sophisticated black-and-white line drawings complement
the narrative.   The author highlights many of the great
achievements of the Incas, such as: "With their engineering ability, the Inca added many miles of canals,
aqueducts, and causeways, which carried water to the
steepest fields.   They put a steady water supply into
Cuzco and even had running water in the Temple of the
Sun and in the emperor's palaces. ...   Archeologists
today marvel at the engineering of the irrigation canals.
Some of them seem to be winding uphill, and yet they
worked perfectly" (p. 87).

Burland, C. A. Inca Peru. Illus. :   Yvonne Poulton.
(Philadelphia: Dufour Editions, 1962, 93 p.) Grades:
4-8.

This book includes very interesting facts about
Peru as it was in the time of the Viracocha Inca about
A. D. 1450.   In a simple and readable text, with small
black-and-white drawings, young readers will learn about
Inca Peru's animals, army, boats, children and school,
clothes and jewelry, farming, food and drink, geography,
gods and religion, government, homes and houses, medi-
cine, metalwork, music and dance, peoples and life,

pottery, spinning and weaving, stonework, towns, and travel.   An example of its simple and straightforward approach to Inca life is the following paragraph that tells about the much-criticized Inca Law: "Inca rule might be hard, but it was so wise that people hardly realized that they had lost all their freedom.   They were sure of their homes and a piece of land on which to grow their food.   If there was a famine the Inca fed them from his stores.   If they needed clothing they had a fair share from the town storehouses, to which they had already given some of their own work.   Everything was so well organized that ordinary people found nothing to worry about" (p. 86).

*Burland, C. A.   Peru Under the Incas.   (New York: G. P. Putnam's Sons, 1967, 138 p.)   Grades: 9-12.

This is an outstanding introduction to the work of the Incas written in an easy-to-understand, direct style, with excellent photographs in color and black-and-white.   It describes the Inca land and its inhabit-ants, their administration, divine beliefs, social life, geographical expansion, arts, and the Inca today.   The author's vivid style and ability to recapture Inca times can be best demonstrated by the following paragraph which tells of the life of the ordinary Inca: 'It is strange that we know so little of the ordinary life of the people in Inca times.   The reason is mostly that the Inca people displayed a stern dislike of representa-tional art.   The few surviving legends and tales give a picture of a basically gay people who did not take life as seriously as their architecture would lead one to think.   The excellence of home-made textiles and cera-mics shows that there was a creative happiness avail-able for most people" (p. 95).

Caldwell, John C.   Let's Visit Peru.   (New York: The John Day Company, 1962, 95 p.)   Grades: 3-8.

An interesting description of ancient and modern Peru through 1960 that may be used as an introduction

to its people, geography, and history. It also offers
some amusing facts about Peru, such as "the story of
the llama. " Black-and-white photographs add interest
to the text, although a few are obviously dated. The
tone is sometimes condescending: "...our government
is trying to help Peru so that its resources can be developed" (p. 71); and the last paragraph: "Let's hope
that more Americans, individually--or through our gov-
ernment--will help our neighbors in Peru to a better
way of life. This has been a matter of great importance to the United States; for our security and happiness will be threatened if the peoples of Latin America
turn to communism as a way of solving their problems"
(p. 95).

*Carpenter, Allan. Enchantment of Peru. (Chicago:
Children's Press, 1970, 90 p.) Grades: 5-10.

In a very readable, direct manner the author describes Peru yesterday and today (1969). Attractive
photographs and maps complement the description of
Peru's geography, earliest civilizations, people, natural treasures, as well as of the contrasts of life in
Peru among the very rich and the very poor. It is an
especially good introduction to the Inca Empire. The
author emphasizes important achievements of the Incas:
"The Inca Empire has been called the best working so-
cialistic government in the history of the world" (p.
32). The book contrasts the life of the Incas with that
of modern Peruvians: "The lives of the Sierra Indians,
also, have changed little over the centuries. In fact,
in many ways, Peru is less advanced than it was during
the Inca times. The Inca people cultivated much more
of the land, and their people had more to eat than the
Indians do now" (p. 62). And, "Not only did the Inca
Empire have more extensive agriculture than present
day Peru, but it also had a more extensive highway
system. Inca roads reached many places where modern roads still do not go" (p. 77).

Cavanna, Betty. Fancy Free. (New York: William
Morrow and Company, 1961, 256 p.) Grades: 7-10.

Fancy Jones, the sixteen-year-old daughter of an archaeology professor, decides to go with her father on an expedition to Peru as the lesser of two evils. The other members of the expedition are full of excitement and repeatedly convey their fascination with the culture of the Incas, but Fancy's only interest in life are handsome boys; and her attitude regarding boy-and-girl relationships is not too progressive: "It was her private opinion that girls shouldn't be too clever or knowledgeable, because boys didn't like that type. The male animal, Fancy was convinced, needed to feel superior" (pp. 16-17).

Amid the thrilling background of Inca villages and ruins, llamas, the Andes, and archaeological findings, the author highlights Fancy's short romance, which taught her that "first impressions can be misleading."

*Clark, Ann Nolan. Secret of the Andes. Illus.: Jean Charlot. (New York: The Viking Press, 1952, 130 p.) Grades: 5-8.

Through the sensitivity of a great author the reader is introduced to the marvelous Inca culture. Cusi, an Indian boy, and Chuto, the old Inca llama herder, have maintained many of the values and traditions of the Incas: their love of music; their affection toward llamas; their pride in their history; and their reverence toward nature and their temples. Two well-known Inca legends are beautifully interspersed with Cusi's growing-up dilemmas.

Eiseman, Alberta. Candido. Illus.: Lilian Obligado. (New York: The Macmillan Company, 1965, 30 p.) Grades: K-2.

Through Paco, a boy who lives high in the mountains of Peru, and Candido, a white llama, the reader is introduced to the habits and customs of the Indians of Peru and their faithful llamas. Line drawings depict scenes of the mountains of Peru, a rope bridge, a herd of llamas in a pasture, and market day at a village.

*Glubok, Shirley. The Art of Ancient Peru. (New York: Harper & Row, 1966, 41 p.) Grades: 3-10.

Through the magnificent art of ancient Peru the reader is introduced to the pottery, textiles, jewelry, and architecture of the Chavin, Mochica, Nasca, Tiahuanaco, Chimu, and Inca cultures. Simple explanations and striking photographs should entice young readers to explore the outstanding achievements of ancient Peru.

*Glubok, Shirley. The Fall of the Incas. Illus.: Gerard Nook. (New York: The Macmillan Company, 1967, 114 p.) Grades: 3-6.

The author has abridged and adapted two sixteenth-century documents, one by the Inca Garcilaso de la Vega and the other by Pedro Pizarro, a cousin of the well-known conquistador. The story of the rise and fall of the Inca Empire includes real and imaginary pre-Empire Inca rulers; the period of the Inca Empire, which began around 1438; an eyewitness account of the Conquest; and commentaries of Inca life, customs, laws, beliefs, and rules of conduct. The Inca drawings add authenticity to the narrative. Good readers who would like to increase their understanding of the Inca civilization will find this book most enlightening.

Halsell, Grace. Peru. (London: The Macmillan Company, 1969, 133 p.) Grades: 7-12.

Very good introduction to Peru (as of 1968) that includes: the land, early Peruvians, the Conquest, the colonial period, art and culture of early Peru, the Revolution and after, Peruvians today, rural life, life in Lima, cultural life, the economy, a tourist's paradise, foreign relations, and the future. In simple language it describes important aspects of Peru. For example: "In Inca days the roads were used only for foot travel, since at that time the Indians had neither the wheel nor horses. Yet the Spaniards reported that

their roads were so splendid they could ride their
horses six abreast and could even have used carriages.
'Nothing in Christendom,' exclaims one of the conquerors, 'equals the magnificence of the Inca roads'" (p.
23). And, "many experts say the Peruvian was the
foremost weaver of all time. The Indians made cloth
as early as two thousand years before Christ" (p. 44).

Harris, Leon A. Young Peru. (New York: Dodd,
Mead & Company, 1969, 64 p.) Grades: 3-6.

Through very good black-and-white photographs
the reader is introduced to the children of Peru--at
home, at school, at work, and at play, in the cities
and in the country. Unfortunately, the author emphasized Peru's poverty in most of the pictures as well as
in the text: "Many boys work as limpiabotas (boot-
blacks), competing fiercely for business" (p. 34); "Indians from the mountain regions keep coming into the
cities.... There are no houses or jobs for them so
they end up in the slums where they live in the streets
until they can manage to get a small shack made of
bamboo or mud bricks" (p. 43). There are countless
pictures of destitute children in the slums shown in
various forms of privation and need.
It is indeed regretful that the author insisted on
emphasizing only one side of Peru.

*McMullen, David. Mystery in Peru: The Lines of
Nazca. (Milwaukee, Wisconsin: Raintree Children's
Books, 1977, 48 p.) Grades: 4-6.

Jim Woodman, a modern-day explorer, "is
searching for the reason an ancient people [used] to
carve lines and pictures in the sun-baked Nazca soil"
(pp. 5-6). Black-and-white and color photographs show
huge designs (as seen from the air) of monkeys, spid-
ers, condors, and strange spirals which were carved
into the ground at least 2,000 years ago. The author
believes that "ancient balloonists ... gazed down at these
Nazca lines some 2,000 years ago" (p. 47); there are,

however, other theories that try to explain why the ancient lines were drawn.   This is an interesting introduction to the study of Inca culture.

Molloy, Anne.   The Girl from Two Miles High.   Illus. :
Polly Jackson.   (New York: Hastings House, 1967,
184 p.)   Grades: 4-6.

Phoebe and her father lived in a mining camp in the Andes Mountains of Peru.   The author briefly describes Phoebe's life with her father and their servant Rosita.   After her father's sudden death, Phoebe is sent to Maine to live with her grandmother.   Phoebe felt lonely and afraid.   She had never lived in the United States; she had never made her bed; and she had never gone to school.   Phoebe's gradual adapting to life in the States, as well as her feeling of belonging in her new world, are depicted.   However, Phoebe and her life in Peru are never truly described for the reader.   Only a few superficial observations are mentioned about Peru.   For example: some Americans believe that "all Indians were ignorant and thievish" (p. 23); and, "In the 'barriadas, ' the great slum city where Rosita lived, all the houses looked alike to Phoebe, the same pathetic mixture of materials--flattened-out oil cans, flimsy rush mats, weathered boards" (p. 32).

*Moseley, Michael E.   Pre-agricultural Coastal Civilizations in Peru.   (Burlington, North Carolina: Carolina Biological Supply Company, 1978, 16 p.)   Grades: 9-12.

Simple maps, charts, diagrams, and an interesting text describe the historical, artistic, and economic development of the coastal Andean civilizations and their maritime foundations.   It tells about the Preceramic sites of Rio Seco and El Paraiso, which were excavated in the mid 1960s, and their impressive architecture: "The corporate labor that went into El Paraiso ranks as prodigious by the standards of any preliterate civilization.   That this great undertaking drew its principal support from a maritime economy is monumental testimony to Peru's uniquely rich marine resources" (p. 15).

Pendle, George. The Land and People of Peru. (New York: The Macmillan Company, 1966, 89 p.) Grades: 5-9.

This is a very interestingly written book that describes the history, geography, and economy of Peru through the early 1960s.

The author's British perspective is obvious and refreshing, in his narration of incidents of life in Peru. in the nineteenth and twentieth centuries. The following is an example of his comments regarding the Peruvian government of the early 1960s: "One of the fundamental characteristics of Latin America generally--and Peru is no exception in this respect--is that people are so easily carried away by words. When an eloquent politician has announced what he will do, the mass of the public applaud the words and go home feeling that what has been said has already been done" (p. 87).

The author succeeded very well in conveying the problems of Peru, as well as in describing the distinctive and impressive characteristics of the Inca and Spanish cultures that have influenced Peru.

Pine, Tillie, and Joseph Levine. The Incas Knew. Illus.: Ann Grifalconi. (New York: McGraw-Hill Book Company, 1968, 32 p.) Grades: 3-6.

This book is divided into three parts: it briefly describes what the Incas knew; it explains that knowledge in today's terms; and it tells young readers what they may do to use that knowledge. The most interesting part tells about many things that the Incas knew and did. It tells how they: built suspension bridges and roads, made a calendar, invented a cooking stove, made maps, developed a way of keeping records, and built stone houses without cement.

*Wilder, Thornton. The Bridge of San Luis Rey. Il-
lus.: Amy Drevenstedt. (New York: Grosset & Dunlap Publishers, 1927, 235 p.) Grades: 9-12.

This is the sad story of five travelers who died
when "the finest bridge" in all Peru broke on July 20,
1714. Wilder's beautiful prose narrates the lonely and
solitary lives of the five people who will be remembered only by those who loved them: "There is a land
of the living and a land of the dead and the bridge is
love, the only survival, the only meaning" (p. 235).
Many people of colonial Peru are represented in this
story: The Marquesa de Montemayor, a wealthy and
aristocratic woman; Esteban, a scribe; Uncle Pio, an
artist; Camila Perichole, a well-known actress; and
others that lived in Peru during the years of its artistic
and wealthy renaissance.

BOOKS REVIEWED IN THIS CHAPTER:

*Baumann, Hans. Gold and Gods of Peru. Translated
   by Stella Humphries. (New York: Pantheon, 1963,
   201 p.) Grades: 9-12.

Bleeker, Sonia. The Inca, Indians of the Andes. Illus.:
   Patricia Boodell. (New York: William Morrow and
   Company, 1960, 150 p.) Grades: 4-6.

*Burland, C. A. Inca Peru. Illus.: Yvonne Poulton.
   (Philadelphia: Dufour Editions, 1962, 93 p.) Grades:
   4-8.

*Burland, C. A. Peru Under the Incas. (New York:
   G. P. Putnam's Sons, 1967, 138 p.) Grades: 9-12.

Caldwell, John C. Let's Visit Peru. (New York: The
   John Day Company, 1962, 95 p.) Grades: 3-8.

*Carpenter, Allan. Enchantment of Peru. (Chicago:
   Children's Press, 1970, 90 p.) Grades: 5-10.

Cavanna, Betty. Fancy Free. (New York: William
Morrow and Company, 1961, 256 p.) Grades: 7-10.

*Clark, Ann Nolan. Secret of the Andes. Illus.: Jean
Charlot. (New York: Viking Press, 1952, 130 p.)
Grades: 5-8.

Eiseman, Alberta. Candido. Illus.: Lilian Obligado.
(New York: The Macmillan Company, 1965, 30 p.)
Grades: K-2.

*Glubok, Shirley. The Art of Ancient Peru. (New
York: Harper & Row, 1966, 41 p.) Grades: 3-10.

*Glubok, Shirley. The Fall of the Incas. Illus.: Ger-
ard Nook. (New York: The Macmillan Company,
1967, 114 p.) Grades: 5-10.

Halsell, Grace. Peru. (London: The Macmillan Company, 1969, 133 p.) Grades: 7-12.

Harris, Leon A. Young Peru. (New York: Dodd,
Mead & Company, 1969, 64 p.) Grades: 3-6.

*McMullen, David. Mystery in Peru: The Lines of
Nazca. (Milwaukee, Wisconsin: Raintree Children's
Books, 1977, 48 p.) Grades: 4-6.

Molloy, Anne. The Girl from Two Miles High. Illus.:
Polly Jackson. (New York: Hastings House, 1967,
184 p.) Grades: 4-6.

*Moseley, Michael E. Pre-agricultural Coastal Civiliza-
tions in Peru. (Burlington, North Carolina: Carolina Biological Supply Company, 1978, 16 p.)
Grades: 9-12.

Pendle, George. The Land and People of Peru. (New
York: The Macmillan Company, 1966, 89 p.)
Grades: 5-9.

Pine, Tillie, and Joseph Levine. The Incas Knew.
Illus.: Ann Grifalconi. (New York: McGraw-Hill
Book Company, 1968, 32 p.) Grades: 3-6.

*Wilder, Thornton.   The Bridge of San Luis Rey.   Illus.:
    Amy Drevenstedt.   (New York: Grosset & Dunlap
    Publishers, 1927, 235 p.)   Grades: 9-12.

PUERTO RICO

Puerto Rico is the easternmost island of the Greater Antilles, about a thousand miles southeast of Miami, Florida. The island, which measures about a hundred miles from east to west and thirty-five miles from north to south, is smaller in size than Connecticut. Puerto Rico has mountains that run the entire length of the island; agriculture is therefore concentrated on the coastal plains. Puerto Rico's principal exports are sugar, rum, tropical fruits, and cement.

Most Puerto Ricans are of Spanish descent. About one-fourth are of African descent and mulattoes. Because Spain controlled the island for more than 350 years, its influence is still evident in the people's language, religion, and customs. Puerto Rico's largest cities are San Juan (the capital), Bayamón, Ponce, Carolina, and Mayagüez. Spanish architecture combines with modern buildings to give Puerto Rican cities a distinctive atmosphere.

Puerto Rico has many problems as a result of its overcrowded living conditions. (The island is even more densely populated than Japan.) Housing has long been a problem; many people live in crowded slums in the cities. As a result, many Puerto Ricans move to New York City and other cities in the United States in search of better homes and jobs. Nevertheless, a new pattern of migration appeared in the 1970s, in which Puerto Ricans left the mainland to return to the island.

The citizenship status of Puerto Ricans is associated with the commonwealth status of Puerto Rico.

Since 1952 Puerto Rico has been a commonwealth of the United States, which means that the island is self-governing but is bound to the United States by allegiance to its Constitution and to its President. Puerto Rico is represented in the U.S. Congress by a Resident Commissioner from the island, who can introduce measures, vote in committee, and speak on the floor of the House of Representatives, but not vote.

Puerto Ricans are United States citizens, yet they do not vote in U.S. elections if they live on the island. If they live on the mainland, however, Puerto Ricans are subject to state and federal taxes and do have the vote.

The following books will introduce students to Puerto Rico and to Puerto Ricans who live on the island and on the mainland. (Asterisks indicate noteworthy books.)

*Barry, Robert. Ramón and the Pirate Gull. (New York: McGraw-Hill Book Company, 1971, 36 p.) Grades: K-3.

Ramón, a young boy who lives in Ponce in Puerto Rico, was very surprised when he saw a bright red gull. His mother wouldn't believe him, and neither would his friend Miguel, nor anyone else--that is, until they see a picture in the post office with a sign saying that "'If you have seen a red sea gull, you must report it to the Marine Research Station in San Juan'" (unnumbered). So, Ramón takes the rare gull to San Juan in an exciting taxi ride in a "público." Amusing line drawings complement the story.

*Belpré, Pura. Once in Puerto Rico. Illus.: Christine Price. (New York: Frederick Warne and Co., 1973, 96 p.) Grades: 2-6.

A delightful collection of seventeen Puerto Rican popular tales and legends that tell of the island's early history and its well-known customs and beliefs. It includes short and simple tales about pre-Columbian Indians, the Spanish conquistadores, the English attack of 1797, as well as Puerto Rico's charming animal tales. A joyous introduction to the people and history of Puerto Rico through a superb native storyteller.

*Belpré, Pura. Santiago. Illus.: Symeon Shimin. (New York: Frederick Warne and Co., 1969, 31 p.) Grades: 1-4.

Santiago, a young Puerto Rican boy, is anxious to show to his friends in New York City pictures of his favorite pet hen, Selina. An understanding teacher and a sensitive mother combine their efforts to tell the children happy things about Puerto Rico. Simple story that should evoke in all children an appreciation for the memories of one boy who left his home to come to New York City.

Binzen, Bill. Carmen. (New York: Coward-McCann, 1969, 42 p.) Grades: K-2.

Carmen is a little girl from Puerto Rico who moves to New York City with her family. She misses her home and her friends in Puerto Rico. Realistic black-and-white photographs and a brief text show Carmen alone in New York City on a rainy day wishing she had a friend to play with. One day she sees another girl in a building across the street and they became good friends. So, "When tomorrow came, it was raining once again. Rain, rain, rain. But Carmen didn't care, and neither did Liza" (unnumbered). All the photographs show life in a poor neighborhood in New York City.

Blue, Rose. I Am Here. Yo Estoy Aquí. Illus.: Moneta Barnett. (New York: Franklin Watts, 1971, 42 p.) Grades: K-3.

A trivial attempt to describe the sad feelings of a Puerto Rican girl who now lives in the United States: Spanish music "made Luz think of her homeland, Puerto Rico, where it was always warm and you never needed a heavy coat" (unnumbered). And, "There were no leaves on the trees outside the school. Luz thought of the green leaves on the trees in Puerto Rico, and she started to cry all over again" (unnumbered). The teacher encouraged the children to play a little game, and when all "the children said, 'Yo estoy aquí,' Luz felt very special and proud" (unnumbered).

A few Spanish words and the mention of "rice with beans and her favorite chicken dish that her grandmother made" (unnumbered), and other superficialities are supposed to display the author's sensitivity to the problems of minority children.

*Bowen, J. David. The Island of Puerto Rico. (New York: J. B. Lippincott Company, 1968, 134 p.) Grades: 7-12.

This is a very informative and readable view of Puerto Rico, with an emphasis on the way of life as of 1967. The author highlights the problems and important contributions of Puerto Rico by sensitively describing the following: population density; folklore, music, and food with Spanish, Indian, and African elements; strategic location at the easternmost end of the Antilles; Spanish domination and "the absentminded rule of the island by the United States during the early years" (p. 91); the "imperialism of neglect" of the United States in Puerto Rico (p. 93); the success story commonly referred to as "Operation Bootstrap"; and the advantages and disadvantages of remaining a commonwealth. Interesting black-and-white photographs complement the narrative.

Brahs, Stuart J. An Album of Puerto Ricans in the United States. (New York: Franklin Watts, 1973, 79 p.) Grades: 4-9.

The story of Puerto Rican Americans on the island and on the mainland is simply narrated and illustrated with black-and-white photographs. It starts with the history of Puerto Rico and continues with the reasons for migration to the United States. It explains the meaning of "commonwealth status" and clearly states that "when Puerto Ricans come to the mainland, they enjoy full citizenship--including the right to vote and the requirement to pay taxes" (p. 28). The book emphasizes several times that Puerto Ricans have suffered various forms of discrimination in the United States and that "because of this, the Puerto Ricans are often forced into second-class citizenship. Puerto Ricans have not been aggressive in fighting for and demanding their rights until recently" (p. 41). "There is a growing demand for power for Puerto Ricans to run their own affairs and rule their own destinies" (p. 71).

The author ignores the Spanish rule in Puerto Rico when he states: "It was in America that the Puerto Rican first learned the sad fact that people often are classified by the color of their skin" (p. 56).

Brau, M. M. Island in the Crossroads, The History of Puerto Rico. Illus.: Herbert Steinberg. (New York: Doubleday and Company, 1968, 108 p.) Grades: 7-12.

A readable account of the history of Puerto Rican people from the island's discovery and Spanish conquest until its status as a U.S. Commonwealth. It includes well-known facts about Puerto Rico's history, such as Sir Francis Drake's defeat: "The defenders had reason to be proud. Only a handful of men, they had turned back England's mightiest seadog" (p. 28); the differences of opinion among Puerto Rico's leaders; and the island's economic problems under U.S. rule in 1902: "...the island's economy continued to go down. More and more property owners were almost bankrupt, and more and more U.S. companies were taking advantage of the situation to buy off properties for the cultivation of sugar" (p. 83).

Buckley, Peter. I Am from Puerto Rico. (New York: Simon and Schuster, 1971, 127 p.) Grades: 5-8.

 Federico, a young boy who lived in New York City, is told by his Puerto Rican parents that they will return to live in Puerto Rico. Federico is very unhappy; he likes New York "a lot more than Puerto Rico because a lot more happens in New York" (p. 5). Federico's experiences with his family and arrival in Puerto Rico are described in the first person, but there is a lack of genuine Puerto Rican feelings in the narrative. As in describing Federico's grandfather: "'Once in a while if your grandfather has had too much beer, he can be nasty, but he's a good man. He isn't drunk often...'" (p. 20). A grandson writing like this about his grandfather?
 Through a good Puerto Rican friend Federico learns to love his new home. They enjoy playing games, swimming, fishing, and many new activities that Federico had never experienced before. His father was very surprised at the change and told him that 'he was surprised that I hadn't kept bothering him about the broken TV tube. 'In New York that's all you ever did when you were in the house'...'" (p. 88).
 The story ends by Federico stating: "...I am glad I am here now. I really am! I want to stay here!" (p. 127).
 This story offers several interesting views about Puerto Rico, but it is definitely not a Puerto Rican's view.

Campion, Nardi Reeder. Casa Means Home. Illus.: Rocco Negri. (New York: Holt, Rinehart and Winston, 1970, 134 p.) Grades: 4-7.

 Through the feelings of Lorenzo Benitez, a poor Puerto Rican boy who lives in New York City, the author preaches to young readers about the greatnesses of Puerto Rico and New York. After a short trip to Puerto Rico Lorenzo's feelings about himself are completely changed: "'...I will be an American first, last, and always, but I am a Puerto Rican, too. I un-

derstand that now. And I'm proud of it, too'" (p. 122).
Lorenzo's mother is enthralled to own "the electric
icebox and the stove and the TV and--and...'" (p. 5),
as well as being ecstatic about a telephone: "'What a
wonderful thing is a telephone! In Puerto Rico no one
ever called us up because we had no telephone. Here
almost everyone has a phone'" (p. 5).

And, obviously Lorenzo is disturbed about his
grandparents' house in Puerto Rico: "Instead of a
bathroom with modern plumbing, he had to brush his
teeth at the kitchen sink and go to the toilet in a smelly
little house in the back yard" (pp. 88-89). An absurd
story that misunderstands people and cultural differences.

Colman, Hila. <u>Girl from Puerto Rico</u>. (New York:
William Morrow and Company, 1961, 222 p.) Grades:
7-12.

Colman is a concerned author, as evidenced by
her writings for young adult readers. She truly sym-
pathizes with the problems and interests of teenagers.
Unfortunately, she has a complete disregard for cultural differences. In this book she portrays Puerto
Ricans from a very limited perspective: She describes
a pretty girl from Puerto Rico as "'a real Spanish
beauty'" (p. 26); but according to the author Puerto
Rican girls don't even know how to dress; they look
vulgar: "In Puerto Rico you all look so lovely, but up
here--well, I guess the clothes are different!'" (p.
161). And, obviously all Puerto Rican men are big
"machos": "Like a great many men, especially Latin
Americans, Mr. Marquez was both sensitive about his
physical prowess and proud of it. He did not like to
be reminded of any lack of skill..." (p. 45).

The author tried to write a story about the conflicts that a Puerto Rican girl experiences when she
moves to New York City, but her story results in an
insult to a group of people that don't appreciate these
kind of generalizations: "'You're getting the disease
of the Puerto Ricans ... the I-don't-care attitude" (p.
177).

*Colorado, Antonio J. The First Book of Puerto Rico.
Rev. ed. (New York: Franklin Watts, 1972, 67 p.)
Grades: 7-12.

This is an outstanding introduction to Puerto
Rico by a Puerto Rican who truly loves his country and
who is anxious to describe its beauties. In a very
simple manner the author tells about the island and its
people, early history, politics and economics, cities,
as well as giving other important facts about Puerto
Rico as of the late 1960s. Attractive black-and-white
photographs complement the easy-to-read text.

Fleischman, H. Samuel. Gang Girl. Illus.: Shirley
Walker. (New York: Doubleday and Company, 1967,
143 p.) Grades: 5-8.

Maria, a fourteen-year-old "bad" Puerto Rican
girl, lives with her mother, brother, sister, and dread-
ful stepfather in a slum in New York City. From the
beginning the author overstates a tragic situation.
Maria's mother is constantly complaining: "'All I've
got is trouble. Trouble and children, and they are
just more trouble....'" Maria is unhappy: she is rejected by her stepfather and ignored by her mother.
She joins a gang that is called, unfortunately, "Spanish
Ladies." After a brief stay at a Youth House, a fight
with another girl, and a robbery involving the death of
a "bad" boy, Maria becomes a "good" girl. She thinks:
"'if this can happen, anything can happen. You might
really get to college. Why, who knows, I might even
get to be a nurse. Anything can happen...'" (p. 143).
This is a melodrama with Puerto Rican characters.

Gray, Genevieve. The Dark Side of Nowhere. Illus.:
Nancy Inderieden. (Minnesota: E. M. C. Corporation,
1977, 40 p.) Grades: 4-7.

This is a story about the New York blackout of
November 9, 1965. It includes an attempted robbery,

in which the burglar was caught by men in the neighborhood, and the birth of a baby, in which the neighbors,
including Tony Diaz, a young boy, kindly cooperated.
It is indeed unfortunate that the author "forced" the
characters to act, look, talk, and think with only negative Puerto Rican characteristics. For example, when
Eloise wanted to become a nurse Papa and Mama were
very upset because, "in the Diaz family, girls weren't
supposed to be nurses.... Earning a living was for
men. Women stayed home and raised kids" (p. 3).
Mr. Padilla speaks very poor English, and Lennie's
mother is constantly borrowing things from the neighbors. The author's only positive statements refer to
the beautiful sight of New York City when the "rising
moon shed a misty glow over the darkened city" (p.
19), and to the tiny baby boy which was born at home.

Hearn, Emily. Around Another Corner. Illus.: Edward Malsberg. (Illinois: Garrard Publishing Company, 1971, 40 p.) Grades: K-2.

Peppino, a young boy, was full of pep one bright
morning. He was anxious to work like a man and of-
fered to help a delivery man, a mailman, a painter, a
window washer, a policeman, a lifeguard, and many
others; but, unfortunately, he was too small to help.
Finally he sees Joe, who is picking up litter. Joe
does need help: "Peppino was a happy boy. Joe
needed him, and he was working like a man" (p. 40).
The illustrations depict scenes of New York City
with a few store signs and posters in Spanish which are
supposed to give the story a Puerto Rican flavor. The
word "cervesa" [sic] is misspelled.

Keats, Ezra Jack, and Pat Cherr. My Dog is Lost!
(New York: Thomas Y. Crowell Company, 1960, 40
p.) Grades: K-3.

This is the story of Juanito, an eight-year-old
boy from Puerto Rico, who was miserable because:
"now he was in a new home, with no friends to talk

to.   For Juanito spoke only Spanish.   And, to make
him feel even lonelier ... his dog was lost" (unnumbered).   So, he decided to look for his dog by himself.
He looked in many places in New York City, and finally
he asked for help.   Many people helped him look for
his lost dog.   At last he found his dog: "Juanito was
too happy to say a word.   He and his new friends took
Pepito home" (unnumbered).

Kesselman, Wendy.   Angelita.   Photos: Norma Holt.
(New York: Hill and Wang, 1970, 66 p.) Grades: K-4.

        Angelita, a young Puerto Rican girl, is shown
in her beloved beautiful Puerto Rico enjoying her life
"in a house high in the mountains" very close to the
sea.   When Angelita and her family move to New York
City, everything was so different: "Their apartment
was crowded and dark.   Her mother was always busy
with the baby.   Her father worked all day long" (unnumbered).   "She couldn't run wherever she wanted the
way she had in Puerto Rico. "   Black-and-white photographs contrast Angelita's life in a beautiful island
with the harshness of life in a New York City slum.
When finally Angelita finds her Puerto Rican doll, she
thought "about Julio and wondered why he had brought
back her doll.   Was it because Julio missed the mountains too, the mountains far away in Puerto Rico?"
(unnumbered).

Key, Alexander.   Flight to the Lonesome Place.   (Philadelphia: The Westminster Press, 1971, 192 p.)
Grades: 5-9.

        Ana María Rosalita, a girl from Santo Domingo,
and Ronnie Cleveland, a mathematical boy-genius, are
too lonely fugitives who end up in Puerto Rico in very
unusual circumstances.   The author included "hechiceras"
(sorceresses) and "the spirits of the indios" to add a
Puerto Rican touch to this story of magic and adventure.
A fantasy story that might appeal to enterprising young
readers, even though Puerto Rico is only superficially explored.

Kurtis, Arlene Harris.   Puerto Ricans from Island to Mainland.   (New York: Julian Messner, 1969, 86 p.)   Grades: 6-10.

Written in chronological order beginning about 50 B.C., this book tells the history of the Puerto Rican people until 1968.   In a simple, easy-to-understand manner the author explains: the Spanish-American War, in which "Puerto Rico along with other territories was ceded, or given, to the United States" (p. 31), as well as the importance of the island's location to the United States; the great migration of Puerto Ricans to the United States in 1945; the problems of unskilled people with little knowledge of English, and their housing problems in New York City; and the commonwealth of Puerto Rico looking forward, with its many contrasts between new and old.

*Larsen, Ronald J.   The Puerto Ricans in America. (Minnesota: Lerner Publications Company, 1973, 84 p.) Grades: 7-10.

In a textbook-like presentation, this book tells the story of the Puerto Ricans in the United States.   It includes a brief early history of Puerto Rico from colony to commonwealth, the migration to the U.S. mainland, the Puerto Rican experience on the mainland and steps toward a better life there, and individuals and their achievements.   The author seems to be quite optimistic about the future of the island's economy, as well as the gains that mainland Puerto Ricans have made in politics, housing, education, and employment. This is a simple introduction to the Puerto Rican people written in a simple-to-understand manner.   The following is an example of how the author describes a well-known complaint: "Many people in this country accused the Puerto Ricans of coming here solely for the purpose of getting free handouts on the welfare programs.   By and large, this was a cruel and unjust accusation.   In fact, most Puerto Ricans considered it a terrible disgrace to be on welfare" (p. 49).

Lewiton, Mina.   Candita's Choice.   Illus.:   Howard
Simon.   (New York: Harper & Row, 1959, 185 p.)
Grades: 3-6.

    Candita Rivera is a shy eleven-year-old Puerto
Rican girl who finds it hard to adjust to her new life
in New York City.   Fortunately, Candita's teacher,
Miss Singer, has a "beautiful smiling face" and patient-
ly helps Candita learn to speak English.   Candita's difficulties in learning a new language are well described,
but her relationship with her family and her neighbors
are too shallow.   During a stay at the hospital she is
suddenly told by Mama: "Your own mother died, Candita, when you were two weeks old" (p. 107).   But
Candita continues to be a marvelous, sweet, shy girl
who, because she is recently experiencing many successes in her new life, decides to remain in New York
City.

Lewiton, Mina.   That Bad Carlos.   Illus.:   Howard
Simon.   (New York: Harper & Row, 1964, 175 p.)
Grades: 3-6.

    Unfortunately, this story is about a Puerto Rican
family that lives in New York City and Carlos, the son,
who can not tell the difference between right and wrong
or between borrowing and stealing.   Endlessly Carlos
is reminded: "'It is better not to do bad things, Carlos.   It is my advice to you'" (p. 20).   But, what does
Carlos think?:   "'Not I.   I will be a bad guy.   I will
join a gang....'   'You will be caught and you will go to
prison....'   'No, I will escape'" (p. 27).   His father
insists: "I wish to tell you now, Carlos, that bad com-
panions will lead you to disaster'" (p. 78).   His uncle
Jorge tells him: "'Be good.   As you are the oldest,
teach the others to be good also.   The main thing is to
be good and to obey your parents and also the teacher
in the big school.   Then you will make something of
yourself'" (p. 90).   And he must also hear it from his
teacher: "'Do you wish to be good or bad, Carlos?
You have not paid attention all day, Carlos.   In order
to learn you must pay close attention'" (p. 177).

A dull sermon that is not needed by any child, Puerto Rican or not.

Mann, Peggy.   The Clubhouse.   Illus.:   Peter Burchard.   (New York: Coward-McCann, 1969, 71 p.) Grades: 3-5.

Carlos, a Puerto Rican boy who lives in New York City, and José, his younger cousin from the Bronx are happy because they can meet in "Carloses Clubhouse." But, soon they are found by the landlord and are told not to come back into the burned-out building. The author attempted to write a story to "prove that a New York City block can be a warm community and neighbors can be neighborly regardless of differences of races and nationality." This is a marvelous idea; however, this story abounds in tedious characters and uninspired descriptions of Puerto Rican clichés, such as: "The only times José came to visit were when his mother went to the hospital to get another baby" (p. 13) and, "'You know as well as me they don't got Puerto Rican pilots'" (p. 26).

*Mann, Peggy.   Luis Muñoz Marín: The Man Who Remade Puerto Rico.   (New York: Coward, McCann & Geoghegan, 1976, 119 p.) Grades: 7-12.

A well-written biography of Luis Muñoz Marín that highlights Muñoz Marín's relationship with his father, Luis Muñoz Rivera, as well as other important figures in his life. The author emphasizes Muñoz Marín's political achievements and his struggles to improve the economy of Puerto Rico. This book offers young readers an optimistic view of the various economic and social problems that affect Puerto Rico today, through the life of its first governor.

Manning, Jack.   Young Puerto Rico.   (New York: Dodd, Mead & Company, 1962, 64 p.) Grades: 3-6.

Through black-and-white photographs and a brief
text the reader is exposed to Puerto Rico in the 1950s.
After a four-page introduction to the island, Puerto
Rican children and teenagers are shown in a variety of
situations at work and at play: learning to spell, playing games, climbing trees, rehearsing a play, learning
ballet, playing ball, working as shoeshine boys, learning Spanish dances, receiving medical care, going to
high school, learning to sew, acquiring several voca-
tional skills, attending Mass, and learning arts and
crafts.   This is a good view of the Puerto Rico of
more than twenty years ago.

*Martel, Cruz. Yagua Days. Illus.: Jerry Pinkney.
(New York: The Dial Press, 1976, 34 p.) Grades:
K-3.

Adan Riera was born in New York City and had
never been to Puerto Rico.   His Puerto Rican parents
own a bodega in New York City and decide to go to
visit Uncle Ulise's plantation.   Adan has many nice experiences with his family in Puerto Rico: he sees the
beautiful mountains, meets many members of his big
family, picks tropical fruits from the trees, and has
lots of fun during Yagua days.   Two-tone drawings show
scenes of Adan in Puerto Rico.

Masters, Robert V.   Puerto Rico in Pictures. (New
York: Sterling Publishing Company, 1977, 63 p.)
Grades: 6-10.

With black-and-white photographs of the 1950s
and 1960s and an optimistic text, this book briefly tells
about Puerto Rico's history, land, people, government,
and economy.   Most of the information describes Puerto
Rico in the early 1960s; however, the author added a
few paragraphs at the end of each chapter to update its
contents.   Basically, this book is quite enthusiastic
about Puerto Rico's future: "Large shopping areas are
being built everywhere on the island, and supermarkets,
dress shops, drug stores and branches of various Amer-

ican chain stores are becoming commonplace.... High quality marble, limestone, gypsum and industrially valuable sands and clay have also been discovered. Puerto Rico's present economic activity is a striking contrast to its former purely agricultural economy" (p. 54).

McCabe, Inger.   A Week in Henry's World: El Barrio. (New York: The Macmillan Company, 1971,   44 p.) Grades: K-3.

Black-and-white photographs and a brief text depict Henry and his family, who live in New York City in the section called "El Barrio--'The Quarter.' It is an area where dope addicts and drunks stand and lie on most streetcorners. It is a place of poverty and broken families. But to some, like the Colóns, it is also a place of hope" (unnumbered). Henry and his family are a very close, loving family; they play and work together. The children do not have many toys; yet they seem to enjoy playing with what they have. They put on their best clothes to go to Mass on Sunday morning and Henry is hopeful that "Papa will take us on a picnic this afternoon" (unnumbered).

*McKowan, Robin.   The Image of Puerto Rico: Its History and Its People on the Island--on the Mainland. (New York: McGraw-Hill Book Company, 1973,   88 p.) Grades: 6-10.

This is an excellent account of the history of Puerto Rico from its discovery by Columbus until its political problems in 1968. The author should be commended for her well-balanced report of Puerto Rico's history, social problems, and political dilemmas. The following, describing Puerto Rico before the American takeover, is a brief example of the author's direct style: "Half of the island's budget of 1898 went to upkeep of the church and the navy. Nearly three times as much was spent on the church as on education. Eighty percent of the population were illiterate. The majority of the people were abysmally poor" (p. 64).

*Mohr, Nicholasa.   El Bronx Remembered: A Novella
and Stories.   (New York: Harper & Row, 1975, 179
p.)   Grades: 9-12.

  A collection of twelve short stories that depict
the harsh reality of many Puerto Ricans who lived in
El Barrio during the decade 1946-1956.   The dreams,
hopes, tragedies, and everyday struggles for survival
of several Puerto Rican families are narrated in these
varied short stories of strong human emotions: "Shoes
for Hector" describes the feelings of a boy who gradu-
ated with honors and whose greatest wish was to own a
pair of shoes "any color except orange!" (p. 39).
"The Wrong Lunch Line" tells about the close friendship
between a Puerto Rican girl and a Jewish girl that sur-
vived the humiliation and embarrassment of unsympathetic teachers.   "Herman and Alice" narrates the life
of a teenage pregnant girl that agrees to marry a 40-
year-old homosexual man.   "Tell the Truth" describes
the agony and frustration of a Puerto Rican child who
must protect her mother.   Each story will affect the
reader differently, but they all tell about the pathetic
lives of the people of the South Bronx.

*Mohr, Nicholasa.   In Nueva York.   (New York: The
Dial Press, 1977, 192 p.)   Grades: 7-adult.

  In this collection of eight interrelated short
stories Mohr describes in her deeply moving style the
sad, depressing, and difficult life of many people of
New York's Lower East Side.   The characters evoke
sympathy in their apparent hopeless existence.   Old
Mary, who escapes her dreary reality by sipping beer,
is married to Ramón, who spends his wages on drink.
Old Mary explains why she never supported or sent for
her son in Puerto Rico: "'...I got to New York all
right, but I was only here a short while and had another
baby.   And no man wants an extra burden, especially
one that ain't his.   So it went, I had another baby and
soon found myself, alone again, this time with two
small kids'... " (pp. 12-13).
  Yolanda, a high-school dropout, narrates her

poignant dependency on drugs.   Johnny and Sebastian are involved in a seemingly satisfying homosexual relationship that includes constant arguments and frequent outbursts.   And Lali, who just arrived from Puerto Rico, is married to a man one year younger than her father.   These stories are indeed intimate portraits of many Puerto Ricans; tragic, but true.

*Mohr, Nicholasa.   Nilda.   (New York: Bantam Books, 1973, 247 p.)   Grades: 9-12.

   Nilda is Mohr's first novel, in which she poignantly narrates her early life in New York City's El Barrio during the Second World War.   Very sensitively the author describes a life of poverty, humiliation, and prejudice, as well as a few happy occasions at summer camp and with her family in El Barrio.   All readers will certainly be touched by Nilda's unfortunate and seemingly hopeless experiences with cold and unsympathetic adults: welfare workers, teachers, the police, and nuns.   Nilda's encounters with prostitutes, drugs, pregnant teenagers, and a difficult family life are indeed a realistic portrayal of the life of a Puerto Rican child in New York City.

Molnar, Joe.   Elizabeth: A Puerto Rican-American Child Tells Her Story.   (New York: Franklin Watts, 1974, 44 p.)   Grades: 4-6.

   Through realistic black-and-white photographs and a brief text the author tells Elizabeth's story "based on tape recordings of conversations with Elizabeth. "   Scenes that depict Elizabeth in East Harlem at home, on the streets, at school, at the zoo, and at the outdoor market emphasize the squalid and unpleasant aspects in the lives of many Puerto Ricans who live in El Barrio. Elizabeth's dream: "I want very much to live in Puerto Rico.   I keep asking my father--when will we go?   I know he is saving up money for a house there.   It's a house in the country with lots of grass and trees and fields right next to it.   It costs a lot of money.   But my father keeps saving a little every month" (unnumbered).

*Newlon, Clark. Famous Puerto Ricans. (New York: Dodd, Mead & Company, 1975, 162 p.) Grades: 7-12.

As stated in the foreword by Maurice A. Ferré, this book contains "thumbnail sketches of some famous Puerto Ricans." The author emphasizes the hardships that the following Puerto Ricans have had to overcome to succeed in their chosen fields: Carmen Maymi, activist; Roberto Clemente, baseball superstar; Luis Palés Matos, poet; Herman Badillo, U.S. Congressman; Chi Chi Rodríquez, golfer; Luis Muñoz Rivera and Luis Muñoz Marín, statesmen; Teodoro Moscoso, economic planner and developer; Miriam Colón, actress; Julio Rosado del Valle, painter; Concha Meléndez, writer and critic; Justino Díaz, operatic singer; Jaime Benítez, educator; La familia Figueroa, musicians.
The following words in Spanish are misspelled: Felosofía [sic], Latros [sic] (p. 130); importánte [sic] (p. 138).

Reynolds, Mack. Puerto Rican Patriot: The Life of Luis Muñoz Rivera. Illus.: Arthur Shilstone. (New York: The Macmillan Company, 1969, 96 p.) Grades: 5-9.

This book is a lengthy tribute to Luis Muñoz Rivera that will not appeal to young readers because of the unnecessary praise that it bestows on several Puerto Rican heroes, such as Juan Ponce de León, Luis Muñoz Rivera, and Luis Muñoz Marín. It begins with the history of Puerto Rico, starting with the Spanish conquistadores, and proceeds to the life of Luis Muñoz Rivera, with a brief chapter on Luis Muñoz Marín as governor. It describes important incidents in the history of Puerto Rico in an easy-to-understand manner. The following reports the United States' interest in keeping Puerto Rico in 1898: "The Americans had been thinking about building a canal through Panama. If they did it, then they would want Puerto Rico for themselves to help protect the canal" (p. 68).

Rivera, Geraldo. Puerto Rico: Island of Contrasts.
Illus.: William Negron. (New York: Parents' Magazine Press, 1973, 61 p.) Grades: 2-4.

Simple book that explains in direct language basic
aspects about Puerto Rico and its people. It briefly describes the geography, history, culture, and other important aspects about Puerto Rico, such as the meaning
of "commonwealth," "Operation Bootstrap," and the
problems of the Puerto Ricans who have migrated to
the mainland. Simple two-tone line drawings complement the text. However, there are a few mistakes.
For example, all private schools in Puerto Rico do
not teach in English.

Schloat, G. Warren, Jr. María and Ramón, a Girl and
Boy of Puerto Rico. (New York: Alfred A. Knopf,
1966, 46 p.) Grades: 3-6.

Ramón's mother works in a sweater factory in
Puerto Rico. Ramón's father is dead. Black-and-white
photographs and brief text describe a typical day in
Ramón's life: getting up, washing his face, eating
breakfast, reading his books, and going to school.
María's father is a clerk in a store and her mother
works in a sweater factory. María's typical day is also portrayed: eating breakfast, getting dressed, walk-
ing to school, learning in school, eating a school lunch,
and going to church.
Readers should be told that both families repre-
sent lower-income families of Puerto Rico a long time
ago.

Simon, Norma. What Do I Do? Illus.: Joe Lasker.
(Chicago: Albert Whitman, 1969, 38 p.) Grades: K-2.

Consuelo, a little Puerto Rican girl, lives in a
city housing project in the U.S. This English/Spanish
edition shows Consuelo asking, "What do I do?" and
answering her own question throughout a typical day.
She is shown playing with baby, helping mother, going

to the store, going to school, playing with friends, making pictures, eating supper, and going to bed. This book may appeal to children who are learning both languages; however, neither the story nor the illustrations are especially attractive.

*Singer, Julia.   We All Come From Puerto Rico.   (New York: Atheneum, 1977, 71 p.)   Grades: 4-6.

Through black-and-white photographs and a brief text the author describes many kinds of people that live in Puerto Rico today.   The book shows and tells about: grandfather Barcelo's very large finca, where he grows bananas, coffee, oranges, and citron; grandfather Carlos, who raises Pasofino horses and has won a lot of trophies; uncle Tonio, who is a retired mayor of Vieques; Hector's dreams of becoming a professional baseball player; and Legnaly's dreams of becoming a prima ballerina.

*Singer, Julia.   We All Come from Someplace: Children of Puerto Rico.   (New York: Atheneum, 1976, 88 p.)   Grades: 4-6.

Black-and-white photographs and a brief text describe the life of Puerto Rican children from various villages and one city, Mayagüez.   José and Willy introduce the reader to their island; Jonas tells about the Day of the Three Kings; Raquel describes the Christmas holiday season; Sonia and Jolie tell about their life in Mayagüez; Tanto describes the life in Puerto Real, a fishing village; and José and Willy explain about life in Ensenada, where "almost everybody in one way or another is affected by the sugar.... Either they grow the sugar or cut sugar or load the cut cane onto trailers, or they work in the mill" (p. 72).

Speevack, Yetta.   The Spider Plant.   Illus. :   Wendy Watson (New York: Atheneum, 1965, 154 p.)   Grades: 4-6.

Carmen Santos is a twelve-year-old girl from Puerto Rico. She has a very understanding mother and a hard-working father. Their move to New York City seems to be a relatively easy experience, as " 'there are good people everywhere' " (p. 61). But, when the family had to move to a new apartment, Carmen and her brother get involved in an unhappy incident with a policeman that was not easy to explain. Carmen and her brother feel unwanted in the new neighborhood. But Carmen's amazing talents with a spider plant and the kindness of her Girl Scout leader make life in New York City a wonderful joy for all the family. I am afraid the author simplified too much the difficult experiences of Puerto Rican families who move to New York.

Sterling, Philip, and María Brau. The Quiet Rebels. Illus.: Tracy Sugarman. (New York: Doubleday and Company, 1968, 114 p.) Grades: 6-10.

Through the lives of four Puerto Rican leaders who played important roles in the political life of the island, the reader is exposed to the history and problems of Puerto Rico, from Spain's rule in the fifteenth century to the elections of 1964. Brief biographies tell of the achievements and goals of the following Puerto Rican patriots: José Celso Barbosa, who after 1898 favored statehood for Puerto Rico. Luis Muñoz Rivera, who was elected President Commissioner in Washington and fought for Puerto Rican self-government. José de Diego, who saw Puerto Rico's goals as being independence and autonomy, and Luis Muñoz Marín, who became the first elected governor of the island in 1948 and constantly struggled for the improvement of people's lives.

*Thomas, Dawn C. Mira! Mira! Illus.: Harold L. James. (New York: J. B. Lippincott Company, 1970, 45 p.) Grades: K-3.

Ramón and his family arrive in New York City full of excitement and joy at seeing their relatives in

New York, who owned a big car.   But Ramón's greatest expectation was that "tomorrow he would see the
snow" (p. 24).   Mother was very understanding; she
promised: "'I am going downtown with your Aunt Rosita.   I must buy you a suit for the snow.   I must buy
you boots and a warm cap.   And, of course, I will not
forget gloves so that you can make 'snowballs'" (p. 26).
Ramón has a very good time playing in the snow with
all the children, even though he did not have the proper
clothes and he got sick.   Line drawings of well-dressed
children and adults depict happy Puerto Rican families
in New York City.

Thomas, Dawn C.   Pablito's New Feet.   Illus. :   Paul
Frame.   (New York: J. B. Lippincott Company, 1973,
63 p.)   Grades: 1-3.

        Pablito, a young Puerto Rican afflicted with po-
lio, is described as a weak boy amid a "typical" large
Puerto Rican family.   Accepting the popular misconcep-
tion about Puerto Rican women, the author describes
grandmother as a fragile and helpless person: "Grandmother Rivera dared to think of going against the words
of Grandfather!" (p. 16).   So, when Grandfather Rivera
made the decision to operate on Pablito's feet: "The
apartment exploded with the noise of guitar strings and
slaps on the back and kisses and good wishes" (p. 19),
with the appropriate illustration of a "typical" Puerto
Rican family and a man playing a guitar.   The author
tried to write about the loving support of a large family; however, this is a ridiculous story in an unrealistic
setting.

Tuck, Jay Nelson, and Norma Coolen Vergara.   Heroes
of Puerto Rico.   (New York: Fleet Press Corporation,
1969, 136 p.)   Grades: 7-10.

        This is a collection of eleven brief biographical
sketches of the following heroes of Puerto Rico: Ramón
Power Giralt, Rafael Cordero y Molina, Ramón Baldor-
ioty de Castro, Ramón Emeterio Betances y Alarcón,

Segundo Ruiz Belvis, Ramón Marín Solá, Engenio María
de Hostos, Luis Muñoz Rivera, José Celso Barbosa,
José de Diego y Martinez, and Luis Muñoz Marín.
Each biography tells about the early life and important
political achievements of these well-known Puerto Ricans
in approximately eight pages.   Unfortunately, the author
writes monotonously and repetitively about the lives and
contributions of these famous Puerto Ricans.   These
biographies are not an interesting introduction to Puerto
Rico's history and heritage.

*Weeks, Morris, Jr.   Hello, Puerto Rico.   (New York:
Grosset & Dunlap, 1972, 164 p.)   Grades: 7-12.

This is a most comprehensive and well-balanced
report on Puerto Rico up to 1971.   It is especially
good in focusing on the identity problems of many Puerto Ricans and on the nagging question of the future political status of Puerto Rico: It considers the pros and
cons of remaining a commonwealth, becoming a state,
or working toward independence.   It includes chapters
on San Juan, the island, the differences in lifestyle,
well-known Puerto Ricans, a historical overview, recent economic achievements, and the problems of many
Puerto Ricans who live in New York City.   In discuss-
ing the dilemma of the identity question of young Puerto
Rican painters, the author quotes a painter who stated:
"'We don't know who we belong to.... The Latin
Americans want us to show with the North Americans.
The North Americans tell us to show with the Latin
Americans.   We're always told by the people down here
to paint like Puerto Ricans, but nobody knows what
Puerto Ricans paint like!'" (p. 83).

Williams, Byron.   Puerto Rico: Commonwealth, State,
or Nation?   (New York: Parents' Magazine Press,
1972, 232 p.)   Grades: 9-12.

This is an emotional history of Puerto Rico that
describes its early inhabitants, the Spanish conquest and
colonization, the United States occupation, and the Puer-

to Ricans in the United States. The author condemns the United States for many of its attitudes and policies toward Puerto Rico since the nineteenth century. For example: "...the United States first inherited from England and then developed on its own a contempt of and an animosity toward everything Spanish" (p. 125).

The author presents various arguments that support Puerto Ricans' positions regarding independence, commonwealth status, or statehood, but his major concern is to demonstrate the ineptness of the U.S. government, which has left the island vulnerable to "exploitation by private Anglo-American business interests"; even "under its own constitution it [Puerto Rico] does not yet have as broad an acceptance from the United States of its right to shape its own destiny as was expressed by Spain in the Autonomous Charter of 1898" (p. 177).

The author ends by quoting a bitter complaint: "...it does seem high time that real notice be taken of the growing militancy and frustration among the people of Puerto Rico" (p. 232). It seems to me that the author is trying to simplify very complicated issues even though he is trying to be objective.

BOOKS REVIEWED IN THIS CHAPTER:

*Barry, Robert. Ramón and the Pirate Gull. (New York: McGraw-Hill Book Company, 1971, 36 p.) Grades: K-3.

*Belpré, Pura. Once in Puerto Rico. Illus.: Christine Price. (New York: Frederick Warne and Co., 1973, 96 p.) Grades: 2-6.

*Belpré, Pura. Santiago. Illus.: Symeon Shimin. (New York: Frederick Warne and Co., 1969, 31 p.) Grades: 1-4.

Binzen, Bill. Carmen. (New York: Coward-McCann, 1969, 42 p.) Grades: K-2.

Blue, Rose. I Am Here. Yo Estoy Aquí. Illus.:
Moneta Barnett. (New York: Franklin Watts, 1971,
42 p.) Grades: K-3.

*Bowen, J. David. The Island of Puerto Rico. (New
York: J. B. Lippincott Company, 1968, 134 p.)
Grades: 7-12.

Brahs, Stuart J. An Album of Puerto Ricans in the
United States. (New York: Franklin Watts, 1973,
79 p.) Grades: 4-9.

Brau, M. M. Island in the Crossroads, The History
of Puerto Rico. Illus.: Herbert Steinberg. (New
York: Doubleday and Company, 1968, 108 p.)
Grades: 7-12.

Buckley, Peter. I Am from Puerto Rico. (New York:
Simon and Schuster, 1971, 127 p.) Grades: 5-8.

Campion, Nardi Reeder. Casa Means Home. Illus.:
Rocco Negri. (New York: Holt, Rinehart, and Winston, 1970, 134 p.) Grades: 4-7.

Colman, Hila. Girl from Puerto Rico. (New York:
William Morrow and Company, 1961, 222 p.) Grades:
7-12.

*Colorado, Antonio J. The First Book of Puerto Rico.
Rev. ed. (New York: Franklin Watts, 1972, 67 p.)
Grades: 7-12.

Fleischman, H. Samuel. Gang Girl. Illus.: Shirley
Walker. (New York: Doubleday and Company, 1967,
143 p.) Grades: 5-8.

Gray, Genevieve. The Dark Side of Nowhere. Illus.:
Nancy Inderieden. (Minnesota: E. M. C. Corporation,
1977, 40 p.) Grades: 4-7.

Hearn, Emily. Around Another Corner. Illus.: Edward Malsberg. (Illinois: Garrard Publishing Company, 1971, 40 p.) Grades: K-2.

Keats, Ezra Jack, and Pat Cherr. My Dog Is Lost!
(New York: Thomas Y. Crowell Company, 1960,
40 p.) Grades: K-3.

Kesselman, Wendy. Angelita. Photos: Norma Holt.
(New York: Hill and Wang, 1970, 66 p.) Grades:
K-4.

Key, Alexander. Flight to the Lonesome Place. (Philadelphia: The Westminster Press, 1971, 192 p.)
Grades: 5-9.

Kurtis, Arlene Harris. Puerto Ricans from Island to
Mainland. (New York: Julian Messner, 1969, 86
p.) Grades: 6-10.

*Larsen, Ronald J. The Puerto Ricans in America.
(Minnesota: Lerner Publications Company, 1973,
84 p.) Grades: 7-10.

Lewiton, Mina. Candita's Choice. Illus.: Howard
Simon. (New York: Harper & Row, 1959, 185 p.)
Grades: 3-6.

Lewiton, Mina. That Bad Carlos. Illus.: Howard
Simon. (New York: Harper & Row, 1964, 175 p.)
Grades: 3-6.

Mann, Peggy. The Clubhouse. Illus.: Peter Burchard. (New York: Coward-McCann, 1969, 71 p.)
Grades: 3-5.

*Mann, Peggy. Luis Muñoz Marín: The Man Who Re-
made Puerto Rico. (New York: Coward, McCann
& Geoghegan, 1976, 119 p.) Grades: 7-12.

Manning, Jack. Young Puerto Rico. (New York:
Dodd, Mead & Company, 1962, 64 p.) Grades: 3-6.

*Martel, Cruz. Yagua Days. Illus.: Jerry Pinkney.
(New York: The Dial Press, 1976, 34 p.) Grades:
K-3.

Masters, Robert V. Puerto Rico in Pictures. (New York: Sterling Publishing Company, 1977, 63 p.) Grades: 6-10.

McCabe, Inger. A Week in Henry's World: El Barrio. (New York: The Macmillan Company, 1971, 44 p.) Grades: K-3.

*McKowan, Robin. The Image of Puerto Rico: Its History and Its People on the Island--on the Mainland. (New York: McGraw-Hill Book Company, 1973, 88 p.) Grades: 6-10.

*Mohr, Nicholasa. El Bronx Remembered: A Novella and Stories. (New York: Harper & Row, 1975, 179 p.) Grades: 9-12.

*Mohr, Nicholasa. In Nueva York. (New York: The Dial Press, 1977, 192 p.) Grades: 7-adult.

*Mohr, Nicholasa. Nilda. (New York: Bantam Books, 1973, 247 p.) Grades: 9-12.

Molnar, Joe. Elizabeth: A Puerto Rican-American Child Tells Her Story. (New York: Franklin Watts, 1974, 44 p.) Grades: 4-6.

*Newlon, Clarke. Famous Puerto Ricans. (New York: Dodd, Mead & Company, 1975, 162 p.) Grades: 7-12.

Reynolds, Mack. Puerto Rican Patriot. The Life of Luis Muños Rivera. Illus.: Arthur Shilstone. (New York: The Macmillan Company, 1969, 96 p.) Grades: 5-9.

Rivera, Geraldo. Puerto Rico: Island of Contrasts. Illus.: William Negron. (New York: Parents' Magazine Press, 1973, 61 p.) Grades: 2-4.

Schloat, G. Warren, Jr. María and Ramón, a Girl and Boy of Puerto Rico. (New York: Alfred A. Knopf, 1966, 46 p.) Grades: 3-6.

Simon, Norma. What Do I Do? Illus.: Joe Lasker.
(Chicago: Albert Whitman, 1969, 38 p.) Grades:
K-2.

*Singer, Julia. We All Come From Puerto Rico. (New
York: Atheneum, 1977, 71 p.) Grades: 4-6.

*Singer, Julia. We All Come from Someplace: Chil-
dren of Puerto Rico. (New York: Atheneum, 1976,
88 p.) Grades: 4-6.

Speevack, Yetta. The Spider Plant. Illus.: Wendy
Watson. (New York: Atheneum, 1965, 154 p.)
Grades: 4-6.

Sterling, Philip, and María Brau. The Quiet Rebels.
Illus.: Tracy Sugarman. (New York: Doubleday
and Company, 1968, 114 p.) Grades: 6-10.

*Thomas, Dawn C. Mira! Mira! Illus.: Harold L.
James. (New York: J. B. Lippincott Company,
1970, 45 p.) Grades: K-3.

Thomas, Dawn C. Pablito's New Feet. Illus.: Paul
Frame. (New York: J. B. Lippincott Company,
1973, 63 p.) Grades: 1-3.

Tuck, Jay Nelson, and Norma Coolen Vergara. Heroes
of Puerto Rico. (New York: Fleet Press Corporation, 1969, 136 p.) Grades: 7-10.

*Weeks, Morris, Jr. Hello, Puerto Rico. (New York:
Grosset & Dunlap, 1972, 164 p.) Grades: 7-12.

Williams, Byron. Puerto Rico: Commonwealth, State,
or Nation? (New York: Parents' Magazine Press,
1972, 232 p.) Grades: 9-12.

SPAIN

Spain, part of the Iberian Peninsula in south-western Europe, shares borders with Portugal and France and faces the Mediterranean Sea and the Atlantic Ocean. Spain has striking high plateaus which rise sharply from the sea. Nearly three-quarters of the country is arid, with less than twenty inches of annual rainfall. Madrid, its capital, is located almost in the center of the Iberian Peninsula.

The Spanish people are 99 percent Roman Catholic. Roman Catholicism is the state religion. The decrees of the Catholic Church govern marriage, divorce, and education.

Spain has a literacy rate of 97 percent, and although income distribution remains far from uniform, the nation has developed a large middle class. In the last few decades the Spanish economy has experienced outstanding growth. It is now ranked as one of the largest industrial powers in the world. Its leading exports are oranges and other fruits, iron and steel products, textiles, wines, mercury, and ships. Tourism is one of Spain's major commercial activities and an important source of foreign exchange. Over thirty million tourists visit Spain each year, making it the leading tourist country in Europe.

The Spanish people are very proud of their cultural heritage. In the sixteenth century Spain was the most powerful nation in Europe, and since then its painters, writers, and musicians, as well as its beautiful architectural styles, have received immense recognition all over the world.

The following books will introduce students to the fascinating history, people, and literature of Spain. (Asterisks indicate noteworthy books.)

Carlson, Natalie Savage. The Song of the Lop-Eared Mule.   Illus.: Janina Domanska. (New York: Harper & Row, 1961, 82 p.) Grades: 4-7.

A ridiculous story about a brown mule named Fedro that pretends to include many attractions of southern Spain through the experiences of a mule. There is a visit to Granada and a description of its beautiful scenery. Through Fedro, the singing mule, the author introduced the classical Spanish hero, the Cid: "My mule can sing an entire ballad about the Cid with every word as clear as glass" (p. 12). And the final insult is to Spanish gypsies: "Do you want to be a stupid, wandering gypsy all your life?" (p. 22). "Why don't you go down into town and beg for money?" (p. 44). "Look sad when you beg. Pull yourself together skinny. Look hungry and poor" (p. 45).
By including a bullfight scene and other Spanish customs, this author achieves only a bad caricature of Spain.

*Cervantes Saavedra, Miguel de. Don Quixote of La Mancha. Translated by Walter Starkie. (New York: New American Library, 1957, 1,050 p.) Grades: 11-adult.

This is an excellent translation of Cervantes's great masterpiece, Don Quixote. It includes a very well written twenty-page introduction that provides the reader with basic background information about this famous novel that has delighted readers for many centuries, as well as very appropriate footnotes throughout the novel that further explain Cervantes's witty and alluring writing style. Not every teenager will have the

interest or stamina to read this long novel, in which
Cervantes makes fun of his former pretensions and ambitions and draws a brilliant portrait of day-to-day life
of Spain. However, mature readers will be enchanted
with Spain's greatest novel, which depicts life as "an
unending dialogue between a knight of the spirit who is
forever striving to soar aloft, and a squire who clings
to his master and strives with might and main to keep
his feet firmly planted on the ground" (p. 15).

*Davis, Daniel S. Spain's Civil War: The Last Great
Cause. (New York: E. P. Dutton & Co., 1975, 174
p.) Grades: 8-12.

In a simple, fast-moving style the author narrates the story of the Spanish Civil War from the perspective of the early 1970s. It describes the infant
Spanish Republic in 1931, the agony of the civil war,
the involvement of the great powers of the world, and
the passion of the warring ideologies--fascism, communism, and democracy. Perhaps the author may be
condemned for simplifying complex factors and issues;
however, this narrative may serve as a good introduction that will not overwhelm young readers. The following is how the author explains Franco's success:
"The secret of Franco's political success, both during
and after the civil war, was his remarkable ability to
play one power off against another and to continually
adjust the delicate political balance of the country so
that all groups would be too weak to challenge him and
too content to want to do so" (p. 123). La Pasionaria's
famous slogan "No paserán!" [sic] is misspelled.

Day, Dee. Getting to Know Spain. (New York: Coward-
McCann, 1957, 61 p.) Grades: 3-6.

Highlights of Spanish history and geography introduce young readers to Spain.
This book needs to be updated. Spain is in the
twentieth century, although the author seems not to
realize it: "You might like to take a trip from one re-

gion to another by riding on a little donkey as Spanish boys do, or in a little high-wheeled cart pulled by a donkey, the way little Spanish girls might do" (p. 24). "Every boy in Spain dreams of growing up to be the greatest bullfighter in the world.   Bullfighting is one of the most exciting things in life to every Spaniard" (p. 45).   "Little Spanish girls ... are more interested in learning how to be good mothers, because every little Spanish girl dreams of marrying and having lots of children" (p. 48).   American young readers should get a more up-to-date account of Spanish life today.

Gidal, Sonia and Tim.   My Village in Spain.   (New York: Pantheon, 1962, 81 p.)   Grades: 4-6.

From the narrow perspective of two authors who are slightly acquainted with Spanish culture, young readers are introduced to a Spanish village in the province of Córdoba.

The book abounds in generalizations that were exaggerations even in 1962.   Antonio, the main character states: "I don't mind having holes in my soles-- they can be patched up--but I have outgrown my sandals, and my toes hurt when I wear them" (p. 8).   Francisco, Antonio's friend states: "A good Spaniard never gets tired of eating garbanzos--especially if he cannot afford anything else!" (p. 18).   And, "Many people in our country cannot read at all.   I almost didn't have a chance to learn to read because I had to start working when I was a little child" (p. 50).

The authors mention a few Spanish authors and the greatness of the city of Córdoba, but they emphasize several times their extreme dislike of bullfights: "I do not like the idea of the bulls being tortured for the pleasure of the audience only... " (p. 58).

*Goldston, Robert.   The Civil War in Spain.   (New York: The Bobbs-Merrill Company, 1966, 210 p.)   Grades: 9-12.

This is an excellent historical narrative of the causes and of events leading up to the Spanish Civil

War and the fall of the Spanish Republic.   A very well
written prologue gives the reader an interesting background to the history and people of Spain.   The epi-
logue reviews the results of the civil war as well as
the political situation in Spain through the 1950s.   The
author's knowledge and objective depiction of people and
circumstances make this an amazing study of Spain.
This is the author's view of General Franco: "In the
chaos of political hatreds which preceded the Second
World War, a cynical world could not believe that
Franco was just what he proclaimed himself to be: a
deeply devout, sternly authoritarian, tradition-minded,
intensely proud Spanish patriot" (p. 113).   And, Franco's "great political insight was demonstrated by his
tour de force in successfully keeping Spain out of the
Second World War, an action for which all Spaniards
remain grateful to this day" (p. 205).

*Goldston, Robert.   Spain.   (New York: Franklin Watts,
1972, 84 p.) Grades: 7-12.

This is an outstanding introduction to Spain until
1970.   In a most appealing manner the author highlights
important characteristics of Spain, going beyond superficial tourist-type interpretations.   Striking black-and-
white photographs and maps complement chapters on the
land and people, the cycles of Spanish history since
1492, art and literature, daily life in modern Spain, and
Spain present and future.   The author's sincerity and
knowledge is evidenced in his depth of understanding of
the changes that are now taking place.   This author
does not want to sensationalize, but to convey a true
portrayal.   This is a sample of his descriptions: "Today, soccer football, basketball, and bowling are far
more popular than the bullfight, and more people are
to be found on the beach than in church on a Sunday
morning" (p. 65).

Goldston, Robert.   Spain.   (New York: The Macmillan
Company, 1967, 132 p.) Grades: 7-12.

This is an outstanding introduction to Spain that emphasizes the economic, political, and social forces that have influenced the country up through the early 1960s. It includes excellent chapters on the Spanish people, the golden age of Spain, ("Over the centuries, no nation has made a greater contribution to the world's artistic heritage than Spain" [p. 63]), the Spanish civil war, and Spanish artists and writers of the twentieth century. This book includes information that is now outdated; for example: "...a middle-class woman in Spain simply does not work; the very thought is slightly scandalous" (p. 48).

*Irizarry, Carmen. Spain, the Land and Its People. (London: Macdonald Educational Limited, 1974. Morristown, New Jersey: Silver Burdett, 1976, 59 p.) Grades: 6-12.

This is an outstanding introduction to Spain written by an author who truly knows the country and the people. It briefly describes important aspects of Spanish personality, history, and customs in short two-page chapters. Drawings, maps, charts, and color photographs complement the author's many views of Spain, which include family life, food, faith and ritual, important monarchs, Madrid, tourism, giants of art and thought, and many others. The following are two examples of the author's forthright style: "Contradiction is the hallmark of the Spanish character. The average Spaniard can be generous to a fault, but intolerant like few men on earth. He will take pride in calling himself an individualist while conforming to the standards of a closed society" (p. 50); and, regarding politics in Spain: "Some Spaniards believe their country should adopt a more open, European system, but most Spaniards do not give any thought to politics. They think all forms of government are corrupt, and are content to enjoy the consumer goods and modern conveniences industrialization has brought" (p. 52).

Loder, Dorothy.   The Land and People of Spain.   Rev.
ed. (New York: J. B. Lippincott Company, 1972,
152 p.) Grades: 7-12.

An overview of Spain that includes several chapters on its early history, the Moors, the Reconquest,
the conquistadores, the Hapsburgs, the Golden Age, the
Inquisition, the Bourbons, rulers from Ferdinand VII to
Francisco Franco, a description of various geographical
areas, and Spain in the early seventies.   The author is
a strong supporter of the role of the Catholic Church in
Spanish history.   Regarding Spanish colonies in the New
World, she states: "No racial barriers were set up
between Spaniards and Indians, and laws passed by the
royal overseers finally forbade slavery....   This offi-
cial attitude of tolerance was more effective than most
of us realize....   Spain was more humane than most
colonial empires; she did less to uproot natives under
her rule than any other European country" (p. 47).   The
author seems to have forgotten the destruction of pre-
Columbian treasures that occurred in Mexico and Peru
during Spain's colonial rule.   About the Inquisition she
states: "...we do explain it to a certain extent by
thinking of it as the longest and most severe case of
an epidemic of the times....   Now and then it tried
writers and painters, though not a single author or
artist is known to have been sentenced to death" (p.
74).   And, obviously, she is making an overstatement
when she says: "Many Spanish boys want to be bull-
fighters" (p. 143).

Madden, Daniel M.   Spain & Portugal: Iberian Portrait.   (New Jersey: Thomas Nelson, 1969, 212 p.)
Grades: 7-12.

This book describes Spain and Portugal in the
1950s and 1960s from the perspective of a seasoned
traveler.   The author has visited Spain many times and
is familiar with the common sites and customs.   The
best part of the book are the black-and-white photographs
of city streets, downtown cafes, shoeshining operations,
training schools, and (unfortunately) the ever-present

donkeys that confirm the author's tourist-view of Spain
and Portugal.   It briefly discusses well-known similarities and differences between Spain and Portugal as well
as the economic and political situations in these countries until 1968.   The author states that "political re-
form in Spain is often likened to a Spanish dance--
three steps forward, two backward" (p. 208).

Martin, Rupert.   Looking at Spain.   (New York: J. B.
Lippincott Company, 1969, 63 p.) Grades: 4-6.

Attractive photographs in color and black-and-
white and a simple text describe a typical tourist view
of Spain.   With the common misunderstandings of the
superficial traveler, the author describes the country,
people, food, important cities, industry, cathedrals,
the bullfight, and other well-known Spanish attractions.
The author elaborates on the Spaniards' unpunctuality
and obviously does not know that siestas are very un-
common in modern Spain.   He writes: "After lunch almost everyone has a siesta.   All activities come to a
halt for two or three hours and Spain comes to life
again only around six in the evening.   If a stranger
happens to be abroad during the siesta he will catch
glimpses of people asleep under a tree or a wall... "
(p. 14).

*McKendrick, Melveena, and J. H. Elliott.   Ferdinand
and Isabella.   (New York: American Heritage Publishing Co. , 1968, 147 p.) Grades: 7-12.

Ferdinand and Isabella's remarkable alliance,
which resulted in a united Spain in the fifteenth century,
is narrated through a simple text and outstanding art
reproductions in color.   The authors explain Ferdinand
and Isabella's successful civil war, their devastating
religious persecution, their bitter campaign against the
Moors, Columbus's relationship with the Spanish monarchs, and their children's intricate marriage alliances
with half of Europe.
The authors might be slightly reproved for ex-

aggerating Isabella and Ferdinand's "happy" marriage;
but the authors' obvious intent to achieve balance in
recounting Isabella's and Ferdinand's reign is well
demonstrated in the following paragraph that describes
Isabella's religious intolerance: "For Spain Isabella is
a symbol of past greatness; subsequent generations in
other countries, however, have found it hard to understand or to forgive her religious policy. Nor can its
motivation be explained simply as religious bigotry.
The Queen was certainly a bigot; dogmatic and even
narrow-minded prejudices were inevitable in a person
of her great piety and zeal..." (p. 125).

*Reeves, James. Exploits of Don Quixote. Illus.: Ed-
ward Ardizzone. (New York: Henry Z. Walck, 1962,
219 p.) Grades: 6-12.

This is a marvelous introduction for young readers to Cervantes's Don Quixote. Reeves has maintained
Cervantes's good humor by depicting in a fluid, simple
writing style Don Quixote's delightful adventures and
knightly absurdities and Sancho Panza's incessant search
for material well-being.
Reeves selected and adapted appealing adventures
of Don Quixote, Sancho Panza, Rosinante, and Dulcinea
and successfully preserved Cervantes's enduring human
spirit. This Spanish masterpiece of a poor gentleman
who tries to relive the heroic days of old by going in
search of adventures in the manner of a knight errant
of medieval romance should be enjoyed by all lovers of
classical literature in the world.

*Resnick, Seymour. Selections from Spanish Poetry.
Illus.: Anne Marie Jauss. (New York: Harvey
House, 1962, 95 p.) Grades: 7-12.

This is an excellent selection of Spanish poems
"that have stood up under the test of time," beginning
with the twelfth-century Poem of the Cid through the
twentieth century. All Spanish speakers should be exposed to these thirty-eight poems, which have been

popular favorites for many centuries.   English transla-
tions have been provided on facing pages "to allow the
reader to enjoy the beauty of the poems without the
problems of translating" (p. 9).   This is a marvelous
introduction to Spanish poetry for all readers in a
pleasing format.

Schloat, G. Warren, and Anson Wilson Schloat.   Fernando & Marta, a Boy and Girl of Spain.   (New York:
Alfred A. Knopf, 1970, 46 p.)   Grades: 3-6.

   Through black-and-white photographs and a brief
text young readers are introduced to a poor Spanish
family whose "father suffered an accident and still cannot work steadily..." (unnumbered).   Twelve-year-old
Fernando and ten-year-old Marta are shown at home
in their city of Granada in southern Spain, at school,
and visiting the Alhambra for the mid-day meal: "She
carries the potatoes home in her own shopping bag
since the storekeeper does not supply paper bags.
Even wrapping paper is scarce" (unnumbered).

Spain in Pictures.   (New York: Sterling Publishing
Co., 1962, 64 p.)   Grades: 4-8.

   A simple introduction to Spain that covers the
land, history, government, people, culture, and economy with many black-and-white photographs.   Some of
the information is definitely dated.   For example,
"Technically, Spain is still in a state of war.   The
decree issued by the Defense Junta in 1936 is still in
effect and it gives Franco unlimited power" (pp. 27-
29).   And, amazingly, it describes the Spanish "flashes
of barbarism, even cruelty, have been noted.   For
example, in their idealizing bullfighting, regarding it
as an expression of the union of life with death" (p.
39).

Treviño, Elizabeth Borton de.   Casilda of the Rising
Moon.   (New York: Farrar, Straus & Giroux, 1967,
186 p.)   Grades: 7-10.

Through the life of Saint Casilda the author narrates a tale about medieval Spain in the eleventh century, when "magicians and mystics, saints and necro-
mancers, knights and kings, princesses and lovers" love
and die for the Saviour of the Christians.   The story
tells about the sanctity and miracles attributed to Santa
Casilda in an atmosphere of magic, faith, and religion.
Few young readers will be interested in the mysticism
and prophetic powers of Casilda's spirit.

*Werstein, Irving.   The Cruel Years: The Story of the
Spanish Civil War.   (New York: Julian Messner, 1969,
178 p.)   Grades: 9-12.

The author has recreated the story of the Spanish
civil war through newspapers and a few personal remin-
iscences of American Veterans of the Abraham Lincoln
and George Washington Battalions, which fought in support of the Spanish Republic.   The bitterness and hatred
of the three-year struggle, which savagely divided the
people of Spain, is reported, as well as the interference
and attitudes of the foreign powers that played such an
important role in defeating the Spanish Republic.
The author emphasizes the well-known fact that
the civil war "was only a rehearsal for the catastrophic
struggle that exploded three years later" (p. 140).   He
describes the beginnings of all-out warfare ("now civilians
were in as grave danger as were soldiers" [p. 150])
and the utter destruction of shattering cities by aerial
attacks.   The infamous attack on Guernica is briefly
mentioned: 'Ironically, there was no military target in
Guernica.   A German pilot later admitted, 'It was an
experiment.   We were trying out new tactics for aerial
assault....   Guernica made a good laboratory'" (p. 151).

*Wojciechowska, Maia.   The Life and Death of a Brave
Bull.   Illus.:   John Groth.   (New York: Harcourt Brace
Jovanovich, 1972, 44 p.)   Grades: 3-6.

Through beautiful line drawings and a simple text
the author explains the feelings of a brave bull: "Its

unending bravery, its pride, one might even say its
Spanish haughtiness, were the very qualities expected
of the Spanish knights!" (unnumbered); its first years
in an endless sea of grass; its feeling when "he discovered himself the owner of a wondrous toy--his
horns" (unnumbered).　And the bullfighter's feelings
about a brave bull:　"...grew to love him for his
courage, for his great mobility, for his immense
strength and his endless wish to attack" (unnumbered).
　　　This is a well-written story that might serve as
an excellent introduction to the art of bullfighting.

Wojciechowska, Maia.　Shadow of a Bull.　(New York:
Atheneum, 1964, 155 p.)　Grades:　5-10.

　　　This 1965 Newbery Award winner is the story of
Manolo Olivar, the son of Juan Olivar, Spain's greatest
bullfighter.　Manolo's fears and feelings of indecision
regarding his own future as a bullfighter are very well
developed throughout the story:　"It seemed that he had
always been afraid.　All his life, always afraid, afraid
of everything.　But what could he do, knowing it?　He
would have to learn to hide it until, until he learned to
be brave.　And he must learn, he knew" (pp. 19-20).
Alfonso Castillo, the famous bullfight critic, helps Manolo make up his own mind by advising him to "'Be what
you are, and if you don't yet know what you are, wait
until you do.　Don't let anyone make that decision for
you'" (p. 147).
　　　The author describes the art of bullfighting and
the life of a bullfighter, but her own negative feelings
about bullfighting emphasize its gory aspects.　For example:　"When he looked again, he felt sick at what he
saw.　The bull had charged one of the horses and the
picador had driven a lance into the bull.　Blood was
running down the bull's side" (p. 37).　And, "'I've already spilled my brave blood.'　He laughed, 'You mean,
you have been gored?'　'Two years ago.　About ten
inches of horn in my right thigh...'" (p. 97).
　　　This is a beautiful story about a boy's personal
struggles but an unfortunate introduction to bullfighting.

Wocjciechowska, Maia. A Single Light. (New York:
Harper & Row, 1968, 149 p.) Grades: 7-12.

    This is a depressing story that unfortunately is
set in Almas, a poor village in southern Spain. A
deaf-and-dumb girl is rejected by everybody, including
her father. She has only experienced a lonely, miserable life, and finding a priceless statue might change
her future. All the characters in this story are indeed
pathetic, evil human beings, and all are Spaniards,
with the exception of the hero, an American traveling
in Spain. The men are lazy and drunk, and life in this
Spanish village is utterly without hope: "Nothing and
no one, would ever change the misfortune, the misery,
the poverty, and the hopelessness that were part of
everyone's life in Almas" (p. 111). And, the people:
"Something was wrong with all of them. They were
maimed, in all the evil ways that poverty and lack of
hope can ruin people" (p. 134).
    What is the only source of hope for the girl?
"He would bring her to the United States, adopt her,
and send her to school. He wanted badly to give her
a chance at a decent future.... 'In a decent school,
in America, she will learn what she needs to know.
She will have a good life'" (pp. 144-45).

BOOKS REVIEWED IN THIS CHAPTER:

Carlson, Natalie Savage. The Song of the Lop-Eared
    Mule. Illus.:   Janina Domanska. (New York:
    Harper & Row, 1961, 82 p.) Grades: 4-7

*Cervantes Saavedra, Miguel de. Don Quixote of La
    Mancha. Translated by Walter Starkie. (New York:
    New American Library, 1957, 1,050 p.) Grades:
    11-adult.

*Davis, Daniel S. Spain's Civil War: The Last Great
    Cause. (New York: E. P. Dutton & Co., 1975,
    174 p.) Grades: 8-12.

Day, Dee. Getting to Know Spain. (New York: Coward-McCann, 1957, 61 p.) Grades: 3-6.

Gidal, Sonia and Tim. My Village in Spain. (New
York: Pantheon Books, 1962, 81 p.) Grades: 4-6.

*Goldston, Robert. The Civil War in Spain. (New
York: The Bobbs-Merrill Company, 1966, 210 p.)
Grades: 9-12.

*Goldston, Robert. Spain. (New York: Franklin Watts,
1972, 84 p.) Grades: 7-12.

Goldston, Robert. Spain. (New York: The Macmillan
Company, 1967, 132p.) Grades: 7-12.

*Irizarry, Carmen. Spain, the Land and its People.
(London: Macdonald Educational Limited, 1974.
Morristown, New Jersey: Silver Burdett, 1976,
59 p.) Grades: 6-12.

Loder, Dorothy. The Land and People of Spain. Rev.
ed. (New York: J. B. Lippincott Company, 1972,
152 p.) Grades: 7-12.

Madden, Daniel M. Spain & Portugal: Iberian Portrait.
(New Jersey: Thomas Nelson, 1969, 212 p.) Grades:
7-12.

Martin, Rupert. Looking at Spain. (New York: J. B.
Lippincott Company, 1969, 63 p.) Grades: 4-6.

*McKendrick, Melveena, and J. H. Elliott. Ferdinand
and Isabella. (New York: American Heritage Publishing Co., 1968, 147 p.) Grades: 7-12.

*Reeves, James. Exploits of Don Quixote. Illus.:
Edward Ardizzone. (New York: Henry Z. Walck,
1962, 219 p.) Grades: 6-12.

*Resnick, Seymour. Selections from Spanish Poetry.
Illus.: Anne Marie Jauss. (New York: Harvey
House, 1962, 95 p.) Grades: 7-12.

Schloat, G. Warren, and Anson Wilson Schloat. Fernando & Marta, a Boy and Girl of Spain. (New York: Alfred A. Knopf, 1970, 46 p.) Grades: 3-6.

Spain in Pictures. (New York: Sterling Publishing Company, 1962, 64 p.) Grades: 4-8.

Treviño, Elizabeth Borton de. Casilda of the Rising Moon. (New York: Farrar, Straus & Giroux, 1967, 186 p.) Grades: 7-10.

*Werstein, Irving. The Cruel Years: The Story of the Spanish Civil War. (New York: Julian Messner, 1969, 178 p.) Grades: 9-12.

*Wojciechowska, Maia. The Life and Death of a Brave Bull. Illus.: John Groth. (New York: Harcourt Brace Jovanovich, 1972, 44 p.) Grades: 3-6.

Wojciechowska, Maia. Shadow of a Bull. (New York: Atheneum, 1964, 155 p.) Grades: 5-10.

Wojciechowska, Maia. A Single Light. (New York: Harper & Row, 1968, 149 p.) Grades: 7-12.

VENEZUELA

Venezuela, located on the northern coast of South America, faces the Caribbean Sea and the Atlantic Ocean. It has four distinct geographic regions: the Andes Mountain in the northwest; the coastal zone north of the mountains; the plains, which extend from the mountains south and east to the Orinoco River; and the Guyana Highlands, where Angel Falls, the world's highest waterfall, is located.

Venezuela is one of the least densely populated countries of the Western Hemisphere. Most of the population is concentrated in the Andes and along the coast, where Caracas, the capital, is situated. The people are 67 percent mestizo, and the rest are of European, Negro, or Indian extraction. The literacy rate is estimated at 74 percent. Venezuela has many social and economic problems created by its rapid population growth and by its uneven distribution of wealth. There is a large migration from countryside to towns, causing unemployment of unskilled workers in Caracas and other cities.

Venezuela is one of the world's leading oil-producing and exporting countries. Oil accounts for more than 90 percent of Venezuela's exports. It has twelve refineries, including one of the largest in the world, at Amuay, which enables it to export over one-third of its oil directly as refined products. Venezuela is also a major producer and exporter of iron ore. The main agricultural crops are sugarcane, corn, coffee, and rice, but the country must import wheat, corn, and sorghum to be able to maintain an adequate food supply.

The following books will introduce students to
Venezuela and its people.   (Asterisks indicate noteworthy books.)

*Carpenter, Allan, and Enno R. Haan. Enchantment of
Venezuela. (Chicago: Children's Press, 1970, 94 p.)
Grades: 5-10.

    This is a good overview of Venezuela with at-
tractive photographs and maps.   It includes information
current as of 1968.   In a very readable, simple manner
it highlights the difference between this and other countries in Latin America: "Carlos' father is an engineer
in the oil industry.... [He] gets a big salary from the
oil business" (p. 45).   "Venezuela's oil equals about 6
or 7 percent of the total world oil reserves" (p. 64).
"However, about one third of the people throughout the
country are still in need of better housing and living
conditions" (p. 70).   The book also includes chapters
on Venezuela's history, government, people, and culture.

Hudson, W. H. Green Mansions. Illus. : E. McKnight
Kauffer. (New York: The Modern Library, 1916, 254
p.) Grades: 9-adult.

    In the foreword of this "romance of the tropical
forest" of Venezuela, John Galsworthy wrote of W. H.
Hudson that he "is of course a distinguished naturalist,
probably the most acute, broad-minded and understanding observer of Nature, living" (p. vi).   He further
states about this book that in form and spirit it "is
unique, a simple romantic narrative transmitted by
sheer glow of beauty into a prose poem ... it symbol-
izes the yearning of the human soul for the attainment
of perfect love and beauty in this life... " (p. vii).
Perhaps a few young readers might be interested in a
romantic author's interpretation of love and life, as
well as his feelings about the natives of Venezuela in
the late nineteenth century: "It is hard for me to speak
a good word for the Guayana savages.... I regard
them now, and, fortunately for me, I regarded them

then, when, as I have said, I was at their mercy, as beasts of prey, plus a cunning or low kind of intelligence vastly greater than that of the brute..." (p. 15).

Laschever, Barnett D.   Getting to Know Venezuela. Illus.: Haris Petie. (New York: Coward-McCann, 1976, 60 p.) Grades: 3-6.

In a very readable style the author introduces young readers to Venezuela and its people. Simple line illustrations complement an easy text that tells about Venezuela's history; oil drilling; the sights in Caracas; typical dishes; bullfights; the great plains; the jungle; and the economy up to 1962. The author explains important facts about Venezuela and its relationship to the U.S.: "Nearly half the iron bought abroad by the United States is bought from Venezuela" (p. 53).

Nevins, Albert J.   Away to Venezuela. (New York: Dodd, Mead & Company, 1970, 95 p.) Grades: 7-9.

A basic introduction to Venezuela with information current through 1968. It describes Venezuela's history, government, cities, oil, land, education, and the status of the Catholic Church. Father Nevins's interest in the Catholic Church is demonstrated by his concerns in furthering the support of the Church by the Venezuelan people. He states that upper-class Venezuelans show a lack of conviction in religion and that "divorce is high among these people and one survey showed that 70 percent of those interviewed would not permit their children to become priests or sisters" (p. 68). The book includes many black-and-white photographs that unfortunately do not correlate with the text.

Venezuela in Pictures. (New York: Sterling Publishing Company, 1966, 64 p.) Grades: 5-10.

This is a simple introduction to Venezuela's land, history, people, economy, and government until

1963.   Black-and-white photographs complement the
easy-to-read text.   The editors highlight important aspects of Venezuela's history and economy.   For example: "Except for a few gaps, the history of Venezuela
from 1830 to 1958 is a story of dictators, strong leaders who were usually tyrannical and rarely honest" (p.
32); and, "From 1953 to 1958, when Jiménez was dictator, the closing of the Suez Canal to Arabian oil and
other events caused an unprecedented expansion in
Venezuelan oil production and earnings.   The oil companies made more money and dictator Jiménez became
one of the world's wealthiest men by taking so much of
the increased profits that the people were still left
poor" (p. 54).

Wohlrabe, Raymond A. , and Werner E. Krusch.   The
Land and People of Venezuela.   Rev. ed.   (New York:
J. B. Lippincott Company, 1959 [revised in 1963], 120
p.) Grades: 7-9.

        This is a comprehensive view of Venezuela up
through 1958.   It includes chapters on the land, early
inhabitants, exploration and conquest, colonial period,
war for independence, the Venezuelan Republic, Simón
Bolívar, Caracas, seacoast, Maracaibo basin, mountain
country, Orinoco River, the Guiana, holidays, industry,
and recent history.   The authors write with too much
optimism and exaggerate the improvements that have
been made in Venezuela due to the oil revenues:
"Caracas today is a far cry from what it was in the
colonial period. . . .   The hundreds of mud and brick
huts once clinging to the hillsides are gone.   Many of
the hills have been razed.   Low-rent housing projects
of blocks and superblocks of apartments for workers'
families have mushroomed in their place" (p. 56).
This, unfortunately, is not true in Caracas today!
The last two chapters sound more like political propa-
ganda on behalf of the Betancourt administration than
an honest report of the status of Venezuela's economy.
Many Latin American economists would certainly disagree with the authors when they state: "The policy of
spending wisely the huge national income derived from

oil is making Venezuela one of the most progressive countries of South America" (p. 113).

BOOKS REVIEWED IN THIS CHAPTER:

*Carpenter, Allan, and Enno R. Haan. Enchantment of
   Venezuela. (Chicago: Children's Press, 1970, 94
   p.) Grades: 5-10.

Hudson, W. H. Green Mansions. Illus.: E. McKnight
   Kauffer. (New York: The Modern Library, 1916,
   254 p.) Grades: 9-adult.

Laschever, Barnett D. Getting to Know Venezuela.
   Illus.: Haris Petie. (New York: Coward-McCann,
   1962, 60 p.) Grades: 3-6.

Nevins, Albert J. Away to Venezuela. (New York:
   Dodd, Mead & Company, 1970, 95 p.) Grades: 7-9.

Venezuela in Pictures. (New York: Sterling Publishing
   Company, 1966, 64 p.) Grades: 5-10.

Wohlrabe, Raymond A., and Werner E. Krusch. The
   Land and People of Venezuela. Rev. ed. (New
   York: J. B. Lippincott, 1959 [revised in 1963],
   120 p.) Grades: 7-9.

AUTHOR INDEX

Atwater, James D. , 46, 72

Bailey, Bernadine, 5, 18
Baker, Betty, 47, 72, 73
Baker, Nina Brown, 5, 18,
  48, 73
Bannon, Laura, 48, 73
Barry, Robert, 98, 120
Baum, Patricia, 6, 18, 37,
  43
Baumann, Hans, 85, 94
Beck, Barbara L. , 49, 73
Belpré, Pura, 98, 99, 120
Binzen, Bill, 99, 120
Bishop, Curtis, 38, 44
Bleeker, Sonia, 86, 94
Blue, Rose, 99, 121
Borreson, Mary Jo, 7, 18
Bowen, J. David, 28, 30,
  100, 121
Brahs, Stuart J. , 100, 121
Brau, Maria (M. M.), 101,
  117, 121, 124
Broderick, Walter J. , 32,
  35
Buckley, Peter, 102, 121
Burland, C. A. , 86, 87,
  94

Caldwell, John C. , 22, 25,
  32, 35, 49, 73, 78, 83,
  87, 94
Campion, Nardi Reeder,
  102, 121
Carlson, Natalie Savage,
  126, 137

Carpenter, Allan, 22, 25,
  28, 30, 33, 35, 79, 83,
  88, 94, 141, 144
Carr, Harriet H. , 50, 73
Carter, William E. , 7, 18
Cavanna, Betty, 88, 95
Cervantes Saavedra, Miguel
  de, 126, 137
Chadwick, Lee, 38, 44
Cherr, Pat, 105, 122
Clark, Ann Nolan, 89, 95
Clayton, Robert, 79, 83
Colman, Hila, 103, 121
Colorado, Antonio J. , 104,
  121
Cowan, Rachel, 39, 44
Cox, William, 50, 73

Davis, Daniel S. , 127, 137
Day, Dee, 79, 83, 127,
  138
Dedera, Don, 51, 73
Dunnahoo, Terry, 51, 52,
  73

Eiseman, Alberta, 89, 95
Elliott, J. H. , 132, 138
Ellis, Ella Thorp, 23, 25
Emmons, Ramona Ware,
  64, 75
Epstein, Sam and Beryl, 53,
  73

Fisher, John R. , 8, 18
Fleischman, H. Samuel,
  104, 121

145

TITLE INDEX

SUBJECT INDEX

ALARCON, Ramón Emeterio
Betances y
Tuck and Vergara, Heroes
of Puerto Rico, 118,
124

ALLENDE, Salvador
Bowen, The Land and
People of Chile, 28, 30

ARGENTINA
Caldwell, Let's Visit Argentina, 22, 25
Carpenter, Enchantment
of Argentina, 22, 25
Hall, The Land and People
of Argentina, 23, 26
Hornos, Argentina, Paraguay, and Uruguay,
24, 26
Olden, Getting to Know
Argentina, 25, 26

ARGENTINA - Biography
Rink, Soldier of the
Andes: José de San
Martín, 13, 19

ARGENTINA - Economic
Conditions
Williams, Continent in Turmoil: A Background
Book on Latin America,
16, 20

ARGENTINA - Fiction

Ellis, Roam the Wild
Country, 23, 25
Kalnay, Chúcaro Wild Pony
of the Pampa, 24, 26

ARGENTINA - Social Life
and Customs
Carpenter, Enchantment
of Argentina, 22, 25

AZTECS (See also MEXICO-
History-Pre-Columbian)
Beck, The First Book of
the Aztecs, 49, 73
McClintock, Prescott's
The Conquest of Mexico, 58, 74

AZTECS - Fiction (See also
MEXICO-Legends)
Kirtland, One Day in Aztec Mexico, 57, 74

BADILLO, Herman
Newlon, Famous Puerto
Ricans, 114, 123

BARBOSA, José Celso
Sterling and Brau, The
Quiet Rebels, 117, 124
Tuck and Vergara, Heroes
of Puerto Rico, 118, 124

BELIZE
Moser, Central American
Jungles, 81, 83

153